MY PARENTS ARE
GETTING OLDER

RO SAXON and SHIRLEY ANDERSON

With contributions by Liz Lowe, Dr Peter Lynch and
Rosemaree Morgan

Lothian
B O O K S

Thomas C. Lothian Pty Ltd
11 Munro Street, Port Melbourne, Victoria 3207
www.lothian.com.au

National Library of Australia
Cataloguing-in-Publication data:

Saxon, Ro, 1961– .
    My parents are getting older.

  Bibliography.
  Includes index.

  ISBN 0 7344 0265 1.

  1. Aging parents – Care. 2. Aging parents – Family
  relationships. 3. Parent and adult child. I. Anderson,
  Shirley. II. Title.

362.6

Cover design by David Constable
Typeset by Mandy Griffin
Printed in Australia by Griffin Press

Disclaimer
This book is intended as a general guide and is not intended
to replace the services of professional consultants and health-
providers. The authors and publisher cannot be held
responsible for any injuries or misadventure that may result
from the use of information in this book. To the best of our
knowledge, all information is correct at the time of printing.

Acknowledgements

A special thank you to our partners and the wonderful people and organisations who provided support, encouragement, cajoling and information during the development of this book.

Thank you also to those professional associates and colleagues, friends, family members and relatives who read drafts and provided comments.

Further thanks to Matt Golding, who generously provided the cartoons. They are dedicated to his grandfather, Bert Hopgood.

We appreciate the privilege of having worked with many middle-aged and older people, and with both government and non-government health workers and managers, who through their tremendous resourcefulness inspired us to write this book.

Contents

Introduction

Imagine you are a middle-aged man or woman. You might be a teacher, hairdresser, florist, tradesperson, manager or retail worker. You place a high value on family and are committed to balancing work and family responsibilities. Or you may be quite young with a parent or parents who had you late in life. Or perhaps you yourself are past middle age, with parents who have lived a very long time.

Whoever you are, you have recently noticed that your ageing parents are becoming muddled and you are becoming increasingly concerned about their future and how it will affect yours. You feel an overwhelming responsibility to do something and nurture them in their old age but you are not sure what to do or even what can be done. You are not sure how to broach the subject or what help is available. You know that you would rather do something now than wait for a crisis to occur.

Do you have to imagine? Or is this you now?

My Parents Are Getting Older will answer a range of questions to do with your parents getting older, like:

- Are the problems my parents are having normal for older people?
- How can I help them stay as healthy and independent as possible?
- What about when they need help around the house?
- What services are available and will we be able to afford them?
- Are nursing homes the only option for later on?
- How can I help them and keep my own job and family going?
- What can we be doing to plan ahead now?

This book has been written to help the thousands of Australians who may currently, or in the future, be helping their older parents or relatives to manage.

How this book will help you

My Parents Are Getting Older will increase your knowledge about your parents' expectations of you and about aged-care services so that you can be confident in planning the future. It covers the three critical considerations: you, your parents and the aged-care system.

You will be taken step-by-step through broaching the subject with your parents and discussing with them what you are prepared to do (or not to do) to help them and whether this is anything like they are expecting!

You will be able to understand what is happening to your parents as they age, from physical, mental and emotional points of view.

You will learn how to help them maintain their independence and prevent accidents around the house so that they can continue to look after themselves for as long as possible.

You will find out about the roles and responsibilities of the different health professionals who are involved in aged care, and you will be amazed about the range of helpful services that are available.

And finally, you will learn the facts about nursing homes and supported residential care so that you can help your parents in making the right decisions.

My Parents Are Getting Older is written in everyday language to help everyday Australians who are wondering about what the future holds for their ageing parents.

You will be provided with common sense information, practical advice, guidance and the solutions you've been looking for. And because it's written by experts in the field, you know you can rely on and trust the information.

1 They *are* my parents!

Talking about what they might need, their expectations and plans

Yes, they are your parents. And that probably means you feel some responsibility towards supporting them in their old age. Over the past few years you may have noticed them getting smaller and greyer, and now you have begun wondering how they will manage their future and what impact it might have on yours.

Perhaps the older people you are concerned about are not your birth parents; they could be adoptive parents, parents-in-law, step-parents, separated parents, aged aunts or uncles, old friends of the family or neighbours, in fact any older person for whom you feel some responsibility or concern.

In this book we have used the term 'your parents' to cover all those older people. Similarly, when we talk about your parents' 'home', this includes the many different types of accommodation that older people call home, be it houses, townhouses, units, flats, bed-sits or caravans which are owned, shared or rented. Likewise the term 'partner' is intended to cover both married and de facto couple situations. The current government trend in Australia is to provide support services for older people in their homes rather than in institutional settings such as nursing homes. Like people of all ages, older people have individual preferences. Some are fiercely independent and don't want help. Some are happy to have whatever help they need to enable them to stay in their own home as long as possible. Others would prefer to live with other older people and have all their care provided. What are your parents' preferences? Have you discussed them?

Start talking

The starting point is easy: talk about it! Broach the subject with your parents, both together and individually, and discuss it with other family members. Establish the hopes or plans your parents have for their future, and what various family members are prepared to do to help fulfil those expectations, preferably before your parents actually need assistance! This will help avoid the misunderstandings, stress and heartache that often accompany making decisions at difficult times, such as when your parents are ill or injured.

Your first task is to find out what you, your partner, your parents and other significant family members, like your children, want and need. Really listen to what your parents want and establish their expectations by getting answers to the questions below. If you start talking now, everyone can have plenty of time for discussion, to think and plan ahead, and to come to a shared understanding. It is unrealistic to expect all your parents' hopes and wishes to be aired in one conversation. You may wish to take one question at a time over several discussions, rather than trying to cover them all in one conversation!

Questions to discuss:

- Where do your parents want to live when they are older and frailer?
- Do they have any fears or concerns about getting older?
- Are they experiencing difficulties in managing their daily lives now?
- What tasks do they find challenging or annoying now?
- Would they like any help now?
- What sort of help do they think they might need in the future?
- How would they like different family members to be involved?
- Do they anticipate being able to afford some outside help or pay for some services?
- What outside services would they be willing to accept?

The statement 'I do not want help from any of the family' is pretty definite, and if taken at face value lets you off the hook. But if you ask: 'Why not?', you may discover what your parents really want or fear. You may not agree with or like the answers to some of these questions, but at least you will start to understand what your parents are hoping for — that is if you have been listening not lecturing!

Listening in

Set your goal as finding out what your parents want to do in the future. Be determined to be a listener, and you will probably do well. Remember that for this exercise to succeed, you mustn't be a talker, just waiting for the chance to jump in and have your say the moment your parents pause for breath.

Try to write down all you can remember of what your parents said in response to the questions as soon as possible after your talk. This is a simple test of whether you have been listening. If you can't remember much, maybe you were doing all the talking, or you were asking questions that could be brushed aside with a 'Yes' or 'No'. If you did not get much of an idea of your parents' wishes, have another try. By considering your parents' future before a crisis occurs, there is time to find out what they really want to do, and for you to understand their reasoning and their wishes so you can respect their choices and decisions.

Handy hints

The points below will assist you in making these conversations successful. Plan the discussion and think it through in advance, so both you and your parents can make the most of it.

- Let your parents know you are coming to talk about their hopes and needs for the future.
- Eliminate distractions in the room (turn the television and radio off!).
- Sit where your parents can see your face and maintain eye contact.
- Be relaxed and calm — they may be very anxious.
- Lean towards your parents so they can 'see' that you are listening.
- Nod and give verbal encouragement to keep them talking.
- If they both try to talk at once, discourage this by suggesting they talk one at a time.
- If one person has nothing to say, ask them what they think at frequent intervals.
- Check that you have understood what has been said by summarising from time to time, by saying 'do you really mean...?'

Remember, you are just listening to your parents' ideas and wishes at this time, not arguing about the merit of their ideas. Be aware that being given full attention even for a short while can be tiring — and an unusual experience for older people in many families — so do not exhaust your parents by continuing a discussion after they are showing signs of being tired.

Sentence starters

Sentences can be phrased to help open up and promote the discussion, or to limit it!
Good starters are:

- What do you think about…?
- What do you hope…?
- Have you thought about where…?
- Why do you feel that…?
- I would like to hear what you think about…
- Tell me how it would be inconvenient if…
- I really want to know what makes it hard for you to manage the…

Encourage them to expand on their comments and points of view, by using responses such as:

- I didn't know that, does that mean…?
- Go on…
- Really…?

Difficult families

It is best to recognise that in all families, some things are best left unsaid. Having an open and honest family discussion does not mean 'baring it all'. Even though the power ratio between you and your parents may have changed and at last you feel you can tell them a few home truths, don't hijack this opportunity if you want to solve your current problems of their care. Stick to the discussion!

All families are different and you know yours best; not all families are cooperative groups of people who like each other. Almost all families will have their 'sensitive' areas; these can include old disagreements, overbearing members, greedy members and those who will want to opt out. But remember your parents' relationship with those family members is different from yours, so resist discounting the possibility of assistance or participation from any other family member.

If your family relationships are complex and troubled, perhaps it would be worthwhile seeking help from outside the family. This could be a person whose opinion your parents value, like a friend, minister or priest, family doctor, or a professional skilled in the resolution of family difficulties, like a community health nurse, a social worker or mediator.

Some families will have broader concerns to solve, such as when parents will, or should, relinquish management of a family business, share portfolio or income-earning property, and who will succeed them or act on their behalf. Although the intricacies of these concerns are outside the scope of this book, finding out your parents' expectations and plans is still the basic requirement, and talking and listening are the skills required. In these other situations you may need expert legal or financial help to resolve issues and decide who will take responsibility for business and financial decisions.

Fears and concerns

Fear and lack of trust are two great inhibitors of people talking to each other. Recognise that your parents may be extremely fearful of talking about their future. From their point of view, talking about it may make it seem 'real', and make them seem old and frail when they really don't feel that way. Their view of themselves may be very different from yours. The prospect of change can be very frightening for older people, especially if they feel they have not been in charge of such changes. Lack of financial or physical power can make older people feel powerless and fearful.

Older people may not trust the family to let them remain in their own home. Likewise, you may not be confident your parents can manage the risks if they do stay at home.

Be aware that your parents will not tell you about accidents or difficulties if they think this will be used to confirm that they need help.

Two common fears for older people are health and money. A healthy lifestyle can go a long way towards alleviating health concerns, and Chapter 4 provides hints on how you can help and support your older parents to stay as healthy as possible. Older people worry about money in terms of rising living costs, increasing medical bills and being able to afford the sort of care they may want. Like all things to do with money, the key is working out likely future scenarios and planning for them well in advance. This includes finding out about government-subsidised and free services available for older people, which are described in Chapter 6.

Common fears and concerns voiced by *older* people include:

'I have so many memories from living here, I don't want to lose them…'

'They're a different generation, things have changed so much, they don't understand…'

'My biggest worry is my health…'

'I don't want to be a nuisance…'

'I'm worried about how we'll be able to pay for help later on…'

'You're all so busy with your own families…'

'You'll soon get sick and tired of me…'

'To other people it's all clutter and junk — but they're my treasures…'

'Other people are worse off than me — I can manage…'

'I'm reluctant to ask for help because I don't want to take charity…'

'It's frightening living alone…someone may break into the house'

'I might fall over and not be found for days…'

'It can get you down, trying to keep things up to scratch…'

'Being lonely…that's the worst part…'

'That I can get to where I want to go (and afford the taxis)…'

'That I don't end up in some second-rate nursing home…'

'I'm concerned about losing my independence, dignity and self-respect…'

Common fears and concerns of *middle-aged* people about their ageing parents:

'I'm concerned about where they'll live when they can't manage any more...'

'They're pensioners and I know it will be difficult for them financially...'

'If Mum dies first, I'm not sure how Dad will cope with meals and domestic tasks...'

'If Dad dies first, I think Mum would have to live somewhere smaller that requires less maintenance...'

'I'm not sure how I would feel if they wanted to come and live with us...'

'Are they capable of making rational decisions that will affect their future...'

'I think they'll need a lot of help eventually, but I'm not sure where it will come from...'

'I'm really not sure that he should be driving any more but I'm sure he believes he's quite capable or even better than average!'

'I hope that they'll be well cared for wherever they end up living...'

'I hope that if they go into a "home" the staff have enough time to stop and chat and make them feel valued...'

'I'm dreading that just as the kids are off our hands we'll get lumbered with caring for our parents...'

'When the time comes we want to do what's right for them — it's going to be difficult and stressful to make the right decisions...'

Be reasonable and acknowledge that you have concerns about the future, as do your parents. Discuss your parents' fears and your own together. Lead by example; your children may be watching!

Once your parents' expectations and concerns are established, start talking to your immediate family and then other family members. Unless there is a family crisis, do not rush through this phase of finding out what other family members want. The skills of listening and being able to discuss sensitive concerns calmly will be needed from now on in trying to understand everyone's needs and fears, and in marshalling family resources.

If your parents have a doctor who they are comfortable with, it would be a good idea for them to discuss their future plans, and get the doctor's opinion about how realistic their hopes are. Don't be surprised if the doctor's opinion carries more weight than yours! Remember that your parents have the right to try out their own plans even if the doctor or you think they are a bit risky.

Reality check

Just when you are thinking that you have enough to deal with — there's more! It's time to double check just who your parents are. Sure they are 'Mum' and 'Dad', but as individuals and as a couple, who are they? What are you going to have to deal with?

For example:

- Are they a devoted and content couple, supportive of each other?
- Do they live in a situation of continual hostility?
- Is one totally dependent on the other?
- Are both dependent on you or someone else?
- Do you have one parent or two?

- Are they engaged with or disengaged from the family?
- Do you have a bereaved, sad and bewildered parent uninterested in life?
- Are both your parents seemingly uninterested in their future?
- Would you call your parents 'panic merchants' or 'cool, calm and collected'?

Before progressing to the planning stage, and taking into account their personalities and preferences, it is a good idea to work out how realistic the expectations and hopes of your parents are. If they want to continue living in their present home, you will need to look at:

- how they manage now, financially and physically
- whether their health is stable or deteriorating
- whether the house is in good repair, warm and comfortable, or a bit of a wreck
- whether your parents feel they are managing well or whether they are at the end of their tether
- whether they are generally content or sad.

Why not create a checklist or table of your parents' current situation and what they want in the future. If you have both parents, you may wish to do a combined table, with separate comments for your mother and father where relevant. If your parents do not live together or have different views or wishes, you may decide to do one table for each parent, which will give you a good opportunity to really think of them as individuals.

Here is an example:

Aspect	Current	Comment	Wishes	Action/Suggestion
House	Live in own home of 30 years	Reasonable condition, requires work to bathroom; garden increasingly difficult to maintain. House sometimes grubby	To remain living here as long as possible	Help in garden. Bathroom to be renovated with aged care in mind; seek advice on this. Find out about home care or monthly cleaning
Health — Mum	Has arthritis, takes regular medication	Getting slowly worse, cannot walk long distances	To minimise impact of arthritis and control by medication	Contact Arthritis Foundation and find out what they offer
Health — Dad	Generally healthy although has respiratory problems and tires easily	Fairly consistent, although seems worse during winter	To maintain status quo and try and pre-empt winter respiratory illness next year	Talk to the doctor about suggestions and preventative measures
Self care — Mum	Usually well groomed	Reduced sense of smell — sometimes cannot tell when clothes require laundering	To be well groomed and maintain high personal grooming standards	Reinforce washing even though clothes may appear clean
Self care — Dad	Beginning to look thin and neglected	Unaware himself Would be sensitive to criticism about his appearance	To manage at home and still be included in family events	Discuss the situation and tell Dad what help is available, Home Help, personal care, delivered meals
Social contact — Mum	Fully occupied managing the house, finances and self	Mum and Dad spend most of their time together with few outside interests	More social activities, perhaps as a volunteer, or at a social club	Contact local volunteer centre and see what they suggest. Find out about local social clubs

Aspect	Current	Comment	Wishes	Action/Suggestion
Social contact — Dad	Fully occupied managing the house, finances and self	Mum and Dad spend most of their time together with few outside interests	Happy with own company, does not want to do anything with other people	See what may interest him even within the house to keep him mentally stimulated. Perhaps home care, or social visiting services would be acceptable
Security	Deadlocks, fire alarms, gates padlocked	Security could be preventing assistance being easily given. Fire — would they be able to get out?	To feel safe and secure	Check the extent of security. Talk to Dad about leaving keys in the dead-locks at night in case of fire. Family members to have copies of keys
Finances	Pensioners	Additional financial support is provided by the family as required	To be as financially self-reliant as possible possible	Find out about services available to pensioners at subsidised rates

Next steps

Yes, they are your parents and now you will know what their wishes and plans for their future are, as well as having made your assessment of them as people.

2   What about me?

How to help your parents, keep your own job and family going, and not feel guilty

What about me? A very good question! What will all this mean for you and how will it affect your work, play, family and lifestyle? Caring for anyone, in any capacity, takes time and effort. Your future role may include finding out information, providing social support, checking whether your parents need anything or being a part-time or full-time carer. All these factors will impact upon your time, and it's likely that the time required for you in this role will increase as your parents continue to age and need greater support.

At work

Sigmund Freud asserted that work and love were the two essential ingredients for psychological health. Overall our society tends to confer worth through work. Even when people have care responsibilities, it can be beneficial for them to work because of the opportunities for mental stimulation and satisfaction outside the home environment and the caring role. Work can provide a range of benefits such as feelings of well-being arising from the establishment of a working identity, acceptance as a workmate or colleague, and measurable achievements. It may also provide financial resources and an opportunity for relationships with people outside the family. If the workplace is a source of these benefits for you, it is probably unwise to consider giving up your job to take on caring. Instead, direct your energies to organising and monitoring your parents' care. In the long run, your children or those taking responsibility for you later on, will be glad you led by example.

Workplaces vary enormously. Some people are not readily accessible during the working day. Others may not have easy access to a phone at work. Some people may not want their employer to know that they have looming elder-care responsibilities. Other people will have flexible working hours. Some people will be confident of their value and status with their employer, others may feel very insecure. All these things have to be considered when deciding how much you can assist your parents and the timing and kind of help you can give.

Over the past twenty years employers have had to make the workplace more family friendly because of the need to encourage women back into the labour force and because of changing community expectations.

'Elder-care responsibilities' is the term often used to describe the whole range of calls that may be made on a worker's time by ageing parents. You may find it useful to use the words 'elder-care responsibilities' at work as employers are used to hearing about 'child-care responsibilities'. However, elder-care is, of course, very different to caring for children. Child-care is more predictable and has a time span that can be estimated. Other differences are the rewards, the relationship, and employers' attitudes.

Family-friendly workplaces accept and offer a range of practices, many of which are relevant to those caring for elderly parents, such as:

- flexible hours
- job-sharing and part-time work
- elder-care information
- working from home
- flexibility to attend to parents during illness or crisis
- career breaks
- additional leave and unpaid personal leave
- arrangements to check on elderly parents during the day
- support for accessing or organising elder-care.

While the ageing population is projected to increase dramatically over the coming years, in contrast, the potential labour force is projected to grow more slowly. So there will be increasing reasons for employers to want to retain employees. In the future, family-friendly work practices, such as those listed above, will become increasingly relevant for employees who have elder-care responsibilities. It is hoped that employers who have modified their workplace to cater for employees with children will increasingly understand the situation of those with some responsibility for their older parents.

Your approach

You should find out what the situation is at your and your partner's workplace so you can decide who should take primary responsibility for your parents' support during working hours. You may decide not to discuss the situation with your employer and this may mean you need to get other members of your extended family to take some responsibility during your working hours.

Some consideration should be given to the best way to approach your employer without necessarily revealing your own situation. Some suggestions are:

- Start at the lowest level of management or the person you report to and ask about the organisation's attitude to family-friendly practices.
- Find out whether the organisation has any official or documented family-friendly practices and get copies of them.
- Sound out your manager's view of these policies.

If this person is not supportive or has a negative attitude, keep your elder-care responsibilities quiet and proceed to investigate the situation at your partner's workplace instead.

If this organisation has family-friendly workplace practices, then move on to finding out exactly what they are, and think about how they could help you before making a proposal.

Dealing with employers' concerns

It may be useful for you to know what common worries employers have about employees with caring responsibilities. Employers worry about:

- excessive use of the telephone and email during work hours — it is both the time and the fact that the line is being tied up
- unplanned absences
- distraction from the job
- increased time off or sick leave
- staff turnover.

There are practical solutions to reduce your employer's anxiety:

- If you know your employer worries about the phone calls, offer to list the calls and pay, and reassure them that the calls will be as short as possible and that you will make up the time.
- Use your own mobile telephone.
- Tell your employer the strategies you have worked out to

deal with emergencies should they occur.
- Keep unplanned absences to a minimum.
- Tell your employer that your job has a priority in your life and that it is not necessarily 'family comes first' in every circumstance.
- Demonstrate how you can switch back to your work after a phone call involving your older parents.
- Most importantly, do not talk incessantly at work about your parents' latest drama; maintain a professional, responsible and reliable image.

At play

To Freud's elements of love and work for psychological health could be added: play. Even if you are not employed in the paid workforce, do not let this be interpreted by the extended family and your parents to mean you have a lot of spare time and can easily take up a caring role. You still need to keep time for love, unpaid work and play, which may encompass a wide range of leisure activities.

Like your parents, you may find it difficult to avoid becoming socially isolated, depressed and dependent if you have not maintained outside interests. For example, if your only sport, recreation and interest happens to be rowing, then you may be able to pursue it as an active participant well into middle age. When you can no longer row, you may then be satisfied to pursue it as an administrator or coach in a club or rowing organisation. Think of your current 'play' interests and how you can develop them to take you into your later years, and at the same time think of less physically demanding activities that you can add to your interests.

Your health

You may look at your parents and wonder if you will have the same health problems as they have when you are older.

Now is the time to start taking measures to help you keep as fit and active as possible.

It is also the time to think about the stress involved in caring for someone. Fatigue, depression, back problems, social isolation — studies in Australia, Britain and the United States have found that up to 60 per cent of people who care for the aged, sick and disabled suffer from physical and mental illnesses. Other studies show that a carer who continues to work outside their caring role, benefits from the time away, even though they may have a big workload. Carers who work can still have 'time out' and can maintain relationships outside the home. So, by investing in your own health and well-being, you will be doing yourself and your parents a favour.

> GRANDPA & GRANDMA HAVE KINDLY OFFERED TO SOFTEN THE BLOW OF ME MOVING OUT BY THEM MOVING IN!

Social trends

The social trends that have increased the need for elder-care are:

- the shift from institutional care for aged or disabled people to home-based care

- later marriage and the rise in the median age of mothers for first births which can mean that people with ageing parents may still have children at home during a challenging stage of their lives
- divorce rates may mean that a number of people will have more parents to care for than children
- geographic mobility of Australian families means adult children are less likely to be living with or near parents, which complicates any caring arrangement
- both men and women with older parents may be at a very satisfying stage of their own careers and will wish to pursue them
- people with ageing parents could be looking forward to their own retirement and they may take the 'great escape' trip around Australia
- children are likely to rely on their parents for much longer than the previous generation did. Recent studies in Australia show that almost half of all 20- to 24-year-olds live with their parents, and of the 25- to 34-year-olds, 12 per cent are still living at home.

The reality is that middle-aged people could have both elderly parents and dependent children at home.

In 1993, 37 per cent of women in Australia who worked prior to being a carer gave up work as a consequence of it. Recent studies showed that 73 per cent of carers in Australia were women caring for parents. While women are more likely to be carers, they may already have experience in organising home services and child-care, which will have introduced them to publicly funded services. This experience will be useful in organising care for aged parents. On the other hand, men who are juggling elder-care responsibilities with work and other family commitments, such as part-time or full-time parenting, may lack any knowledge of how to access services subsidised by governments. This book aims to help both men and women.

Your goals

So what about me? Whether you are male or female, working or retired, you will have plans and things you want to do, things you want to avoid, as well as hopes and dreams. Before you start committing yourself or your resources elsewhere, indulge yourself and really consider what you want for yourself.

Even if you are not a person who usually writes things down, perhaps it is worth making a few notes now, just so your hopes don't get lost. Write down what realistically you can expect to have for yourself in the next twelve months in terms of, say, relationships, work, leisure, possessions, achievements, health, and financial security. Put them in order of priority.

If you have a relatively simple and stable lifestyle and family, you may be able to think about your own and your family's goals for the next five or ten years. However, if your household is busy and complex and you are only in control of some of the events, a shorter forecast is more realistic. Nevertheless, recording your ambitions is still a good way to focus your thoughts on what is really important. It will help you to decide when a solution outside your own time or resources needs to be found to assist your parents.

Here is such as plan:

Hopes	What has to happen	Want to be in this position by
Enough money to run our house and have an annual holiday	Both keep working until we are 65 years old and keep up superannuation payments Children paying own way	Job security established within next 6 months By the time they finish university
Peace and quiet in the house	Sound proof family room Older children move out Younger children stick to rules about music	Within 3 months Within 18 months Immediately

Hopes	What has to happen	Want to be in this position by
More time and money for leisure activities	Household jobs have to be shared around. Our leisure has to be given some priority	Immediate start, really working in 2 months and continuing
Garden looking good	Develop a less labour-intensive design. Allocate funds to implement the design Budget for regular paid help	Looking good for next Christmas — 6 months away
Lose weight and get fit	Have to really want to do it	By Jane's wedding in the new year — 11 months away

This can be a fun way to raise issues as well as starting to think about your future. When you have finished the table you might like to write your 'life situation' story and, if you keep to the time schedule and plan, how you hope your life will be a year from now. Put your story in an envelope and open it at Christmas time and see if things are happening for you!

So now that you have reviewed your own priorities and goals, and are clear about the wishes and desires of your parents, who else forms part of your immediate or extended family and what can they offer?

Your immediate family

One of the best answers to the question 'What about me?' is 'What about everyone else?'. Who are the other 'players' in your life? Your immediate family includes your partner and family living at home, who need to know that there is likely to be a change in demands on the family because your parents are ageing.

It is important that everyone in your immediate family understands how your family depends on each other to provide the overall resources that you have. You know best how to approach your immediate family. Depending on the age of your children and the ways you usually relate, it may be helpful to write down your immediate family's resources, along with those of your extended family, using a form like the table 'Family and other resources' below. If you and your partner are both working, it is easy for even the most uncooperative adolescent to understand how they will be financially worse off if one of you has to give up work. So spell it out. Let everyone know there will be changes. Everyone will have to contribute — it may not be much initially, but it will be something. Phone calls, dropping in after school, running errands; there are plenty of contributions to be made.

Your extended family

It is also time to start considering the extended family. You may be surprised at how many people will be on this list when you count significant others in your parents' lives such as friends and neighbours. This is especially important if you are assisting your parents from interstate or overseas.

Even if you have an extended family member whose main characteristic is to 'throw money' at problems, don't knock this, use it. Don't disregard members who are the 'social butterflies' of the family; your parents will love outings with them. Don't leave out teenagers or grandchildren; a phone call or card can bring such joy to an older person and brighten their day.

Older people often get great pleasure and pride from being able to say 'I don't need help with the lawns (or the shopping), my grandson or grand-daughter does that', or 'I'm not lonely, my family ring me up all the time'.

Try to make a realistic assessment of what each person could contribute across the range of things your parents need and will accept from family members. Watch out if you feel you really should be writing 'workhorse' as the characteristic against your own name, and start working on sharing the load around!

Family and other resources

Name	Relationship to your parents	Other commitments	Resources	Characteristics	Current contact with parents
Joe	Eldest child of three siblings	4 children under 18; wife works full-time; long working hours — career oriented	2 good cars; large house, no spare bedrooms; some financial surplus ; sociable family, good planners; lives 10 minutes drive from parents	Agreeable and co-operative; peacemaker; sportsman	Christmas and birthday or other family celebration - when arranged by others
Self	Eldest daughter	3 children under 12; works 4 days per week; husband works regular full-time hours	2 cars — one not reliable; small home, tight budget; lives 30 minutes drive from parents	Dutiful, hardworking, conscientious; organises most family social events; works for family harmony	Twice weekly — to do shopping and to keep company
Debbie	Youngest daughter	Working full-time interstate; partnered 2 step-children under 10	Accessible during the day at work	Career orientated; disengaged from family of origin	Cards and phone calls at Christmas, birthdays etc
Richard	Eldest grandson	Year 12 student; competitive team sports	Energy; physically strong	Focus on girl-friend, studies, sport	Usually attends family gatherings
Lilian	Best friend who lives 5 minutes away	Attends same club	Can provide transport to and from club	Long time friend, good emotional support	Weekly

You may have many more useful headings, and you are sure to have lots more people to add. When you have all the family and friends listed, crosscheck this with what has been listed as your parents' needs.

The guilt factor

There are times when we feel guilty about doing something mean-spirited, unfair or illegal and so we ought!

Deciding whether the right thing has been done by another person or by you can be a very subjective judgement. Some of the suggestions in this chapter should help you be more objective and fair in your decisions and actions and to be more reasonable in your dealings with your older parents.

One example is to set objective standards of fairness for any negotiations with your parents. If they or other family members are demanding more of you, say 'No', and try to feel comfortable about it. 'No' can be a very positive word. Especially if saying 'No' means you can say 'Yes' to more of the things you want to do. Being an accommodating person is fine, but if you find yourself saying 'Yes' and feeling angry and put upon, then it is time to learn to start saying 'No' when it matters to you.

When you list the resources or skills of all family members, if you find there are others with the same resources and skills as you, but you are the only one asked to do things for your parents, delegate the task, and don't feel guilty. By knowing your parents and your own interests you will be better able to judge when yours or their

Your guilt score

Give yourself one point for every time you say, 'Yes' to the following questions.
Do you feel guilty if:

- you do not telephone your parents every day?
- you do not visit your parents every week?
- your work takes priority to the extent that you spend less time with your parents than you would like to?
- you do not include your parents in every outing that has other family members attending?
- you forget their birthday?
- you do not want to take them shopping?
- you have more money than they do and spend money freely while they are more frugal?
- you have a better house than they do?
- you don't take their side when others are running them down?
- you are glad to live interstate?
- you feel impatient and annoyed at your parents, or get cross with them from time to time?
- you avoid them or are relieved when plans with them are altered or cancelled?
- you have not invited them over for a meal for a long time?
- you don't want to hear how they are feeling or what has gone wrong today?

interests should come first. Say, 'No', and don't feel guilty.

If you scored 14 points then you probably have a bit of a problem with feeling guilty. On the other hand, if you answered, 'No' to all the questions, then perhaps a little guilt would help you be more caring and thoughtful! A comfortable feeling in relationships tends to come from balancing conflicting demands and desires in order to achieve some sort of a fair go for everyone.

Keep a life by negotiating

Negotiation is a two-way communication designed to help you reach agreement when you and another party each have interests and goals which you want to protect. Negotiating is not about wearing down the other person. Negotiating is about understanding the interests of everyone concerned, like your parents, your family and you, and working out solutions which will bear these in mind.

By now you should know what your parents' hopes and dreams are, and you will have made a priority list for your future. You should also know what your partner and immediate family want and have a good idea of the interests and resources of the extended family.

Be aware that a particular situation can be perceived differently by different people. For example, you may see your parents' home as cluttered with junk and your interest will be to have it cleared out so that anyone coming in can get a clear go at the housework. Your parents may see their home as filled with treasures collected over a long life and their interest will be that if anyone comes in to do the housework they should have respect for their possessions and work around them. So negotiate, remembering to see interests from both points of view. (Later in this chapter there is a negotiation exercise to test your skills.)

How to negotiate

The basic elements for successful negotiation are to:

- separate the people from the problem
- focus on interests not positions (not 'I'm the son and paying for this', or 'I'm the parent and what I say goes')
- discuss and brainstorm a range of possible options
- agree on a minimum standard that evaluation of the result can be based on
- agree on action and responsibilities.

This is of course not as simple as it sounds. But it is good advice and it will work. You have to recognise that emotions will come into it and may run high at times. This is when it will be useful to check if you are sticking to the basic rules above and thus avoiding a fight or a power struggle with your parents or other family members.

There will be some shared interests and some opposing interests. It is useful to recognise that interests will cover the basic human needs for security, economic well-being, sense of belonging, recognition and control over one's life. So determine at the outset that your negotiations with your parents will be fair, because you will endeavour to see their interests from their point of view and you will check how well the solution caters for the basic human needs of your parents and yourself before putting the plan into action.

Because getting help with the housework is usually the start of outside help for older people, it will be useful to look at negotiation skills through the example of the cluttered hard-to-clean house.

A practical example — getting help with the housework

Step 1: *Separate the people from the problem.*

Don't: Decide that your parents are stubborn old hoarders and have to change their ways.

Do: Agree that doing the housework is too physically strenuous for your parents and that it needs to be done by someone else.

Step 2:   *Focus on interests, not positions.*

Don't: Engage in a power struggle as to who is best equipped to make decisions.

Do: Establish your parents' interests in the matter. They may want to reduce clutter by distributing family treasures amongst the family now, or having a clear-out of what they consider rubbish so they can enjoy the treasures. They may not be able to tolerate anything being moved. They may have no interest in having the house cleaned at all. Be clear about what your interests are in the matter. These could be to have the house cleaned because it is not up to the standard you would like to see your parents living in. It may be because you believe that they will jeopardise their chances of fulfilling their wish to continue living in their home.

Step 3:   *Generate a variety of possibilities.*

Don't: Insist on a weekly total house clean and reduction of clutter in the home.

Don't: Have a 'bottom line' of what you will and won't do firmly in your mind from the outset.

Do: Invite a variety of approaches to solving the problem:

  • Clear and clean just the essential rooms such as kitchen, bathroom and toilet regularly and clean the other rooms occasionally or never. Your parents may be able to maintain the other rooms.
  • Pack some treasures into a spare room or a display cabinet for ease of cleaning.
  • Choose a house cleaner who will be tolerant of clutter and work around it.

- Have a 'spring clean' and leave it until your parents want it done again.
- Include 'throw away' lines and joke suggestions like 'we need to have a garage sale' there may be a real message in there.
- Discuss and consider all the ideas put forward.

Step 4: *Agree on a standard for the outcome of your negotiations so you will all know when it is satisfactorily achieved.*

Don't: Take the view that if the house is not as clean as yours then it needs cleaning.

Do: Try to set a standard of house care — a basic minimum that you all agree is adequate. See whose opinion your parents would value if you cannot agree on a necessary standard. Encourage a visit by that person, or a professional to establish what's necessary to help your parents live independently and safely in their own home. Work out together what action and assistance is needed to achieve the basic minimum standard and make arrangements that are fair to all concerned. If you all agree on this but your parents suggest that your wife leaves work so she can do their housework, then fairness has not been achieved and the negotiations are not complete.

Step 5: *Agree on the action and responsibilities.*

Once you have agreed, you will need to decide whether you will access a commercial or publicly subsidised service, and whose job it will be to make inquiries and arrange the service. (See Chapter 6)

What if my parents won't negotiate?

Maybe your family culture has always been 'Father/Mother knows best'. Now they are older you feel it would be unfair to upset that well-established family pattern. Perhaps you cannot see yourselves even starting the negotiations suggested here. While urging you to give it a try, we acknowledge that you know your situation best and that sometimes the other side seems just too powerful, or you have too much to lose if you change the way you have always related. In this situation you should:

- promise yourself you will not agree to something you know you should reject
- try to bolster your self-esteem and make the most of your resources and assets
- clearly establish your interests, hopes and needs and hold on to them
- read this chapter again and see if you really think you cannot negotiate with your parents.

Practice

Like all skills, practice makes perfect. So why not practise using the negotiation techniques above on the story below, even if it involves a minimum of cooperation by your parents.

The story shows a stalemate situation. Could the daughter improve things by using the negotiation techniques listed above, even if her father is not keen on discussing the problem? Think about the following questions:

- How would you separate the person from the problem?
- How would you focus on interests, not positions?
- What possibilities and options can you generate?
- How would you agree on standards for the outcome?
- How would you agree on actions and responsibilities?

——————— *Story* ———————

*M*ARGARET AND HER DAD *got on all right mainly because, until her mum died, Margaret had most to do with her mother. Her dad kept to himself even after he stopped working. Reading books, watching television, studying the form, putting a bet on the races and following the football, just about rounded out his activities. Margaret and her mum were the ones who organised family celebrations, circulated the family news, talked about the grandchildren and mutual friends, exchanged recipes and cheered each other up. When Margaret's mum died, her dad could scrape together a simple meal and that was about all. He was an intelligent man and could have mastered using the washing machine and the vacuum cleaner, but he simply never considered doing either of these things, and he was 79 with severe arthritis and other health problems. At least he had a regular person to cut the lawns, and his garden was low maintenance.*

Margaret's dad wouldn't think of living anywhere but in his home, and during the first few awful months after her mother died Margaret always cooked enough food to take around to her father to reheat. She also brought his washing home and went over at weekends to do the housework. After a year Margaret found herself tired, her husband complaining that they never had time to do anything together, and her children taking advantage of the fact that Margaret was often not at home. Her dad's home was half an hour's drive away and she also had a part-time job, so she did not have any time to do what she wanted to do.

Margaret made enquiries about home-care services at the local government office in her dad's area, and she was told that her father would probably be eligible. Margaret thought it best to talk it over with her dad first. He flatly refused to hear of 'some woman' coming in to do the work in 'Mum's' house. Margaret said that she could not keep doing his housework and he told her not to do it, that he didn't care if the housework was done or not. Margaret cut back on her visits and did less work for her dad, but she was not happy. The once neat and tidy house was becoming grubby. She wondered if her dad was eating properly and she guessed he never changed the sheets on his bed. Whenever Margaret tackled her dad about these things he always said he didn't care and he wasn't having another woman in the house doing the work. If it worried Margaret she could do it for him.

Compare your solution to our suggestions at the end of the chapter. Note that they are sure to be different simply because there are no right answers; there are a number of ways to improve difficult situations.

Do you think Margaret and her dad could live with this solution? Do you think that he would agree? It may not be an ideal solution but it's a start. Margaret's dad and the house would be just about clean enough, Margaret would still be in contact with him, Margaret is doing some things to help, her father is involved with the family, and Margaret has some more time for herself. If her dad becomes unwell or cannot do the things he has undertaken to do, then having negotiated an arrangement once, maybe it will be easier the second time around.

Reality check

Do not expect things to be easy during the phase of your life where your parents are beginning to become a concern and possibly a responsibility of yours. Even if your parents were able to accept and possibly make the changes in their relationship with you — from a child to an adolescent, to a young adult, to an older adult and onto a middle-aged adult — they may not be able to cope with change that makes them dependent on you in any way. In their mind you may now be one of the 'army' of people who are threatening their way of life. You may even become 'an enemy' in their eyes, and this is a sad loss for you both.

Your parents may lose the ability they have had in the past to discuss, adjust, see the merit of a sensible argument, or make wise decisions and stick to them. You need to understand this, but do not expect them to acknowledge it as they may have been willing to do in the past. It is important to understand that the ways in which you previously had discussions may not work now. You need to develop new ways of reaching decisions with your parents. Of course, it should never be by 'telling them' what is going to happen. Even if you are viewed as 'the enemy', do not act like one. This is the time for guiding discussion, offering suggestions and allowing time for thoughts, not ruling things out. Your aim should be to come back with options and lead on to decision making, although this is never easy.

A crisis will often make action necessary and if some guiding and listening has taken place before one occurs, your parents may accept change more easily.

If your parents have been independent and self-reliant all their lives, then becoming more dependent on you is going to be hard to take. On the other hand, some parents are extremely cooperative. They may be sick of the continual struggle of life and gladly agree to do 'whatever you think is best'. Others, who have been dependent on someone most of their lives, are quite comfortable with passing the responsibility on to you. This dependent attitude may annoy you, but it can be less destructive on your relationship than that of the fiercely independent older person.

You have been given some ideas about how your relationship with your parents might change, how to communicate with them, and how to balance the needs of your work, your family, your parents and you.

Housework negotiations: a solution

This solution was devised without further discussion with Margaret's dad who will not discuss the matter at all at this stage. Margaret has 'guessed' some answers from her knowledge of her dad and has come up with an idea to start working on.

Separate the person from the problem.

Dad's OK — it's hard for him, he is lonely and sad. I'll appreciate his problems and won't criticise him.
The problem is that:

- The house is getting dirty and he looks grubby.
- The house is not cleaned regularly.
- Me doing the work is not acceptable to my family.

- 'A strange woman in the house' is not acceptable to my Dad.
- House cleaning is something which needs to be done.
- Money could be allocated to having the house cleaned.
- Paying for house cleaning has not been agreed upon.

Focus on interests not positions.

- Dad is interested in staying in the house.
- I am interested in helping him to continue to live there.
- I am interested in the house being clean and neat.
- I know that Dad is interested in looking after the things that Mum treasured.
- I suspect that Dad would like the house to be as neat and clean as Mum kept it.
- I must give my family more attention.
- I want to have time to do the things I want to do.
- I must not continue to work so hard because I am tired all the time.
- I don't think Dad wants to become a grubby old person.
- I know Dad likes nice things to eat.

Generate a range of possibilities.

- Can anyone else in the family do the housework?
- If the silver was polished and the dusting done would Dad notice the difference?
- Would this encourage Dad to have the house cleaned?
- If Dad were out could he tolerate a person cleaning the house?
- Would an occasional spring clean suffice?
- Would Dad accept delivered meals, or supermarket prepared meals of some sort?
- If Dad got out more often would he begin to realise how grubby his house is?
- Would Dad accept a commercial cleaner or a male cleaner?
- Would Dad accept the family paying for the house cleaning?

- Can Dad learn to do the washing and would he do it?
- Would Dad send sheets and towels to the laundry?
- Would Dad take all the washing to a laundromat that provides a wash, dry and fold service?
- Could Dad could start doing some cleaning jobs himself, eg. the toilet?

Agree on standards for the outcomes.

- I would be happy if the house was clean enough for people to be willing to visit Dad at home.
- I believe Dad would like the house as neat and clean as it used to be.
- I suspect Dad would like to keep up his businessman image of the clean shirt and neat pants.
- If the house was cleaned thoroughly monthly this would satisfy us both.
- Three clean shirts a week would be sufficient.
- Fortnightly bed change would be enough.
- Some purchased meals, some invites out and some scratch meals would be adequate.

Although it is much better if you are able to talk to your parents and hear their point of view on everything, Margaret's dad had shut the door on discussion. She had to work through the first four steps using her past knowledge of her dad and the attitude he usually took towards things. Having got this far without having further discussion, Margaret now has to start her negotiations with her father, by putting up some proposals and dealing with the final step, which is to agree on actions and responsibilities.

Margaret was a bit apprehensive about talking to her dad. She had continued to visit fortnightly and take a few prepared meals but she had stopped doing the housework months ago. The next time she called over with some meals, Margaret did a bit of ground work by polishing the silver, dusting and putting some flowers in a vase. She also asked Dad over to her place for a meal. He was still driving so could make the trip easily.

After another month Margaret was ready to put her proposal. After some encouraging comments, some sympathy about the state of the house and being on his own, Margaret put her proposal:

- Margaret would continue to visit fortnightly and would do the nice touches around the house, like dusting, polishing silver and doing small things that could be seen and enjoyed like flowers in vases, plumping up cushions, throwing out old newspapers etc.
- Dad would purchase some pre-cooked meals, and drive over to Margaret's about fortnightly for a meal, as arranged with her.
- Margaret would continue to provide some home-cooked meals for Dad to reheat.
- Dad and Margaret would change the bed on her visits, fortnightly.
- Dad would take all the washing to a laundromat with wash, dry and fold service.
- Dad would engage commercial cleaners to clean the house monthly, preferably when he was over visiting Margaret or out elsewhere.
- Dad would pay for the house cleaning.
- Dad would clean the toilet and washbasin as necessary.
- Dad would keep up with the dishwashing.

3 Are the problems my parents are having normal for older people?

Understand what's happening to your parents physically and emotionally and what to expect and why

Like many other people in your situation, you may be wondering whether the problems your older parents are having are normal. In fact, most people in the community do not have a clear understanding of what the major distinctions are between normal and abnormal ageing.

What's normal?

While many of the detailed distinctions are a matter of some debate and ongoing research, there are many misconceptions in the community about even the basics of what constitutes normal ageing. Western culture carries with it some deeply ingrained social, physical and mental stereotypes about the aged.

The biblical axiom of 'three score years and ten', with its implication that all years beyond seventy are the exception rather than the rule, is obsolete in advanced Western countries like Australia. Popular television culture abounds in adverse stereotypes of the aged, such as frail, stooped, grey, stupid, immobile, in pain, unattractive, dependent, poor, manipulative.

Ironically, older people themselves may not be immune from believing some of these stereotypes. They grew up in a time when longevity was less common and in an environment where concepts of ageing well were even less developed than they are today.

Your older parents may not have a well-developed understanding of their own ageing. If you can have a better understanding of these concepts, you can assist your parents to age well and learn what is and is not a normal part of ageing.

Why are my parents still alive today and how long are they likely to live?

Life expectancy has dramatically altered over the past twenty-five years. Australia has one of the best life expectancies in the world, usually rated as second only to Japan. Life expectancy refers to the average life expectancy for a baby born today. In Australia the average life expectancy for men is now 76.4 years, and the average life expectancy for women is now 81.8 for years.

To get a better perspective on the extent of ageing in our community, two other sources of information are useful:

• Life tables provide data on age-related average life expectancy. You may be surprised to learn that your ageing parents, if alive and relatively well today, have a statistical likelihood of living well into their nineties!

- For life expectancy in your parents' local area, you can refer to detailed demographic projections from the Australian Bureau of Statistics. This will show the expected numbers of people aged over 70 and over 85 respectively and their likely increase in the future.

Australia now has a significant population of people aged 100 years or more (centenarians) and a recent study revealed that the majority of them are living at home with minimal support services. For a number of reasons our current aged parents may have life expectancies even greater than the current statistical averages suggest.

This is a consequence of the many public health triumphs of the twentieth century. Our elderly parents have lived through an age where:

- premature death and morbidity from infectious diseases have been dramatically reduced
- the incidence of premature death from coronary heart and cerebrovascular disease has been dramatically reduced
- the risk of dying from some form of injury or trauma is lower than ever before
- many forms of cancer can be detected earlier and treated more effectively than ever before in human history.

In addition to the favourable environmental factors that have developed during our parents' lifetimes, there are also some families where a genetic trend to longevity exists.

Thus there is every chance that your ageing parents will live a long time. Both you and your parents will need to take this into account in planning for their future.

What to expect

Having survived into their eighties and nineties, there are three prospects that your parents now face with their continued health and well-being:

- Firstly, they will experience some of the features of normal ageing which will be described shortly.
- Secondly, they may have 'carried' with them into their old age some element of disability from a condition or conditions that they acquired in middle-aged life or earlier. It would not be uncommon for them to be on medication to control conditions such as high blood pressure, heart disease, high cholesterol, diabetes or other endocrine disorder, arthritis or respiratory conditions.

  Advanced ageing itself might then affect what happens to these conditions and how their bodies will metabolise any such drugs. For instance, some medications which previously may have been effective and well tolerated may now cause problems with advancing age. In some cases, the underlying condition will not need the same doses or even the same medications for their control.
- Thirdly, they now become susceptible to some of the conditions that are much more common in older age and in particular the degenerative conditions of the nervous system, such as dementia.

While the risk of your older parents acquiring new age-related disabilities increases with advancing age, in fact many older people will be relatively unaffected by these types of conditions.

The challenge for everyone is to learn how to minimise the risks of age-related disability. In addition, knowing the difference between normal and abnormal ageing, and being able to identify what can be done to maintain normal ageing for as long as possible, are important for your ageing parents and you.

What are the general features of normal ageing?

Although precisely what constitutes normal ageing is a matter for ongoing research, recent studies have assisted our understanding. While avoiding the stereotypes alluded to earlier, we should also be careful not to romanticise ageing, by recognising that there is always some decline.

As people age there is a slow, progressive but moderate decline from the mid-forties onward in a number of physical, sensory and mental capacities, including sight, hearing, reaction time and endurance, and perhaps most significantly, some aspects of cognitive functioning. However, the total decline is often of the order of 20 to 30 per cent of overall function. This decline tends to 'plateau' at about 75 per cent of peak function earlier in life.

The ageing brain

One of the stereotypes of ageing is that you will suffer from dementia, and in particular from Alzheimer's disease. Most people will suffer some minor decline in their thinking and reasoning, but only a minority will be affected by dementia. It is true that dementia is an age-related condition, because the probability that an aged person will be affected by dementia increases with age. Even so, it is the *minority* rather then the *majority* who are affected.

No doubt concern regarding the integrity of mental or brain functioning with ageing is a major concern for you and your parents. The distinction between normal and abnormal ageing and brain function is very complex and usually not clear to most people. One term often used, 'cognitive functioning', refers to mental processes such as a person's ability for understanding, memory, intelligence, perception, intuition, thinking and reasoning.

Recent studies in neuropathology and other disciplines have demonstrated some of the key features of the pattern of cognitive decline associated with *normal ageing*. The first major feature is that some aspects are affected more than others. The second major feature is that older people perform well sometimes and poorly at other times. They are less consistent than younger adults.

Poem

Just a line to say I'm living
That I'm not among the dead
Though I'm getting more forgetful
And more mixed up in my head
For sometimes I can't remember
When I stare at the foot of the stairs
If I'm going up for something
Or I've just come down from there
And before the fridge so often
My poor mind is filled with doubt
Have I just put the food away
Or have I come to take it out
And there are times when it's dark outside
With my nightcap on my head
I don't know if I'm retiring
Or just getting out of bed
So if it's time to write to you
There's no need of getting sore
I may think I have written
And I don't want to be a bore
So remember I do love you
And wish that you were here
But now it's nearly mail time
So I must say goodbye my dear
There I stood at the mail box
My face so very red
Instead of mailing you my letter
I have opened it instead

Author unknown

Intelligence

Neuropsychologists divide intelligence into two types:

- 'crystalline' intelligence — attributes such as long-term memory, general orientation and the capacity to retain general previously learned life skills
- 'fluid' intelligence — attributes like rapid problem solving techniques.

It has been found that crystalline intelligence is well preserved with normal ageing but that there is a slight general decline in fluid intelligence. Both this attribute and the increased variability in intellectual performance will perhaps be recognisable to many adult children of older parents. You may notice that your parents cannot solve problems as quickly as they used to and that they have good and bad days.

Large variability in performance from day to day is also an attribute that people with dementia show, for they have even greater variation in their performance (larger swings) than the normal aged person does.

There are some obvious implications of this for everyday life. You may notice some slight variation in your older parents' mental 'sharpness' from day to day. As this has been documented as a component of normal ageing, its occurrence does *not necessarily* mean that they may be going to develop significant cognitive impairment or dementia. The decline in different components of intelligence is something that will not usually be detectable by relatives and it has few implications for everyday life apart from a slight decline in problem-solving capacity.

Age-associated memory impairment

The first and milder condition that has been described is known as age-associated memory impairment or AAMI. There are three major features of this condition:

- It is a very mild condition and everyday functioning is not significantly affected.
- It is relatively common and recent studies have suggested that it may occur in as many as 40 per cent of people over 70 years old. The same studies also suggest that of the population with AAMI only about 1–2 per cent per year will progress to significant cognitive impairment and/or dementia.

- It is usually characterised by very mild, relatively trivial episodes of intermittent memory loss, such as not being able to remember where everyday articles have been placed at times. However, there are no features of ongoing significant decline in the capacity for routine daily life.

Appropriate health professionals can give basic screening tests for thinking and reasoning, so that your parents and you can be reassured that greater decline, which may be feared, is not occurring.

Mild cognitive impairment

The second and more significant degree of cognitive disturbance is generally known as mild cognitive impairment. This condition is usually characterised by persistent memory loss — short-term memory loss in particular. Generally, other functions and the performance of everyday activities will remain intact. In screening tests of cognitive function, affected individuals score persistently abnormal scores, usually on tests of short-term memory. The phenomenon of relatively intact long-term memory and deterioration in short-term memory is one that may be relatively easily detectable in everyday life and it can, to some extent, be understood and compensated for by mature age children.

Moderate cognitive impairment

There are several important factors relevant to how affected parents with moderate cognitive impairment will continue to function:

- They will generally do better when they are in the familiar surroundings of their own home.
- There is often a big difference in their level of functioning between when they are in their own home and when they are suddenly transferred to a new environment.
- Because of the nature of the condition, they are no longer capable of learning and successfully memorising new information and thus will often have greater difficulties when suddenly placed in a new environment.
- They will often get on surprisingly well if they live with a partner who can compensate for any memory disturbances (assuming that the other partner is cognitively intact). In these circumstances they may be able to continue to live in their own home for a considerable period of time.

Mild, moderate, mild-to-moderate or early dementia?

There is really no well-demarcated point between where mild-to-moderate cognitive impairment finishes and early dementia begins. Rather, the process is one of very slow gradual decline at a rate often so slow that such changes may be not noticed by near relatives, in the absence of specialist assessment. The dividing line is usually determined by formal testing of cognitive functioning using well-established cognitive screening tests.

As moderate cognitive decline advances to become established dementia, further significant functional changes begin:

- Memory will deteriorate to a more problematic extent.
- Disturbances in mental functioning will become more widespread than just short-term memory loss.
- Abnormalities of orientation in time and place, ability to do simple calculations, ability to perform and co-ordinate simple tasks that were formerly done with ease, ability to read, write and comprehend what is written, speaking, and in particular, the ability to speak another language will decline.
- Ability to perform spatial-constructional tasks will decline.
- Often gait (style of walking) will also decline.
- As dementia progresses, there is further deterioration in all these aspects to the extent that the capacity for normal independent living becomes no longer possible.

There are recent developments, such as drug therapies, that make it vitally important that ageing parents are fully assessed in relation to the mild or moderate changes described here. The diagnosis of cognitive impairment or dementia as early as possible is more important than ever.

What to expect from dementia

As dementia affects a person's memory, intellect (thinking), language, behaviour, personality and emotions, one of the most difficult aspects of it is dealing with the early stages when one of your parents, or you, may experience great difficulty in living with, or relating to, the affected person. Often other people fail to acknowledge the problem, or fail to see that there is a problem at all. As a result of a combination of anxiety, forgetfulness and some loss in reasoning ability, some older parents will develop difficult attitudes and behaviours.

Some people suffering from dementia will develop distressing behaviours, such as:

- deciding that you have taken all their money
- ringing you twenty times a day
- ringing you throughout the night
- ringing you again immediately after they have spoken to you
- denying that you have visited or spoken to them when you have
- refusing to accept that they have lost the ability to make decisions about their finances, or where they should live
- failing to recognise you as their son or daughter
- talking constantly about totally nonsensical things
- forgetting how to start doing the most simple things, such as getting dressed.

Story

THANK YOU FOR LISTENING to me the other day when I telephoned you because I was so upset after seeing my mother. I realise now that her move to accommodation where she receives full care was really necessary. You mentioned that your father has dementia and that he has changed in his personality. You told me that he was nasty to everyone and had caused great fights all around the family, which I am very sorry to hear. My mother has not changed in personality at all. She is still her dear self, kind and gentle, well groomed, cooperative and very social. When I visited her last week she became agitated and distressed. I could not work out what was happening at first, then I wondered if she may want to go to the toilet. I took her there she smiled, her usual warm smile, and said 'What are we here for? Just give me a hint, just a clue, and I will be right.' She could use the toilet after given a hint. The awful thing was that she could not think what to do by herself. I could hardly contain my tears and quickly escaped to the car to have a good cry.

If your parents or you are concerned, consult your parents' doctor. Identification of the cause of the problem can lead to better management and assistance for those caring for the affected person. Chapter 5 provides details of the assistance available for dementia suffers and their families.

Emotional and psychological aspects

Contrary to what is sometimes suggested, there is no single psychological disturbance that is totally unique and distinctive to older age. Once again, we need to distinguish between normal ageing and some of the features of abnormal neurological and psychological/psychiatric states in the elderly.

Older people, like all others, are subject to the slight mood changes that are an inevitable part of human experience. Such mood swings are strongly associated with major life changes such as retirement and bereavement, as well as a sense of isolation and loneliness. Obviously older people have more of these experiences than most and thus may experience reactive mood swings more often.

Depression

Significant clinical depression can occur in older people, and it should be clear that this is different from normal ageing. Apart from the profound mood disturbances that characterise this condition, such depression is often associated with physical symptoms. For example:

- loss of appetite and/or loss of weight occurs in some people
- increased appetite with weight gain occurs in other people
- dry mouth, nausea, constipation, or diarrhoea
- lethargy, lack of interest and energy
- sleep disturbances
- general withdrawal from previous activities and interests.

Clinical depression in the elderly is a serious condition and due to the associated suicide risk, it can be life threatening.

With much attention being given to youth suicide in Australia in recent years, it has been overlooked that the other peak age group for suicide is the elderly.

It is important for clinically depressed people to have adequate diagnosis, treatment involving various anti-depressant medications where appropriate, as well as support including, at times, admission to hospital and the use of various therapies. Such interventions are potentially lifesaving.

Physical aspects

Vision

Recent studies suggest that normal ageing is associated with a slight decline in the sharpness of sight known as visual acuity. A degree of long-sightedness (hypermetropia) and the necessity for reading glasses is common.

Despite a good health system in Australia, some recent studies have suggested that there is a significant degree of under-diagnosis and non-treatment of treatable eye diseases due to older persons not getting their eyes examined. While most of these studies have been of populations in residential care, there is a strong suggestion from community-based studies that the situation is similar in the general community.

Eye disease (as distinct from the mild decline in visual acuity associated with normal ageing) is common in the elderly in Australia and some conditions can be considered age related (in that they become more common with advancing age) such as cataract formation, macular degeneration and glaucoma.

Many conditions can be treated very effectively by optometrists and ophthalmologists with either glasses, various forms of surgery or medications such as eye-drops. There are relatively few conditions that cannot be treated, but even then there are a range of visual aids that can be used to assist older people with everyday function. It is thus vital that your elderly parents are encouraged to access adequate visual assessments.

Doing a number of simple things around the house can greatly help in this area. The importance of adequate lighting to help compensate for any degree of visual impairment cannot be underestimated. Often, elderly parents will not be able to change their own light globes safely and so making sure this happens can be overlooked. It is not worth making a false economy of purchasing low wattage globes when higher wattage globes will provide better light to ensure safety from falls and assistance with fine motor tasks.

Some geriatricians and other authorities in the field of vision have some concerns with the use of bifocal lenses in the elderly. Bifocal (and multi-focal) lenses are increasingly prescribed by eye professionals and are extremely useful for those in their late forties and beyond who have different refractory requirements for near and distant vision particularly in the workplace. However, these advantages may be of less relevance to elderly parents who will not usually be in the workforce. In addition, your parents' insight into the changes in refraction patterns in the various parts of their glasses may not be as acute as that of younger users. Thus, they may wear the bifocal lenses for walking on an uneven terrain or even for driving, relatively unaware of, and unable to sufficiently compensate for, the fact that the lower part of their glasses is designed for near vision. There is no doubt that some falls and accidents occur because of this. However, the extent of the problem has not yet been determined. It may be advisable for older people to obtain separate glasses for reading and near vision purposes and for walking and driving purposes, although this may also cause confusion unless the glasses can be easily identified as reading or bifocal.

Hearing

Like many other sensory capabilities, normal ageing produces a minor loss of auditory acuity of the order of 20 per cent. However, more significant degrees of hearing loss are definitely not part of normal ageing! There is possibly no other area of ageing where significant and easily reversible degrees of loss of function are inappropriately attributed to 'just getting old'.

Ironically, the most common form of significant hearing loss in the elderly is also the one that should be the most easily reversible — blockage of the external auditory canal with wax. The external canals can become almost totally blocked because of it and it can cause loss of over 90 per cent of normal hearing. With relatively early assessment and simple treatment this can be reversed, resulting in a dramatic improvement in hearing, functional status and quality of life.

Other causes of profound hearing loss are more common in the elderly, such as otosclerosis and nerve deafness. In these cases, expert evaluation and intervention are indicated and can be of great assistance. If the use of hearing aids becomes necessary, encouragement and assistance for elderly parents are often needed.

Appetite

It is generally recognised that normal ageing is associated with a slight loss of appetite. In addition, a degree of loss of muscle bulk, bone mass and some degree of atrophy of tissues generally, can result in some degree of weight reduction with advancing years. However, substantial weight loss or decreased appetite, particularly if occurring over a relatively short period of time, should not be attributed to normal ageing and could require expert assessment for the possibility of physical or psychological problems.

Unfortunately, such changes are often attributed to 'just old age' even by health professionals and a number of underlying diagnoses, some of which can be well treated, will be missed. Abdominal pain, hernias and abnormal abdominal swellings are never part of normal ageing and when these occur they should be properly evaluated.

You may have an important advocacy role for your parents should you get the impression that their concerns about their health are being discounted.

Toilet talk

Constipation is another issue about which the barriers between normal and abnormal function are often not clear. Older people can have a slight tendency to constipation for a variety of simple reasons including a decreased fluid intake, decreased dietary fibre because of eating less fruit and vegetables, and decreased activity. Prevention and reversal of this can be achieved by the correction of these risk factors. More significant degrees of constipation should not be regarded as normal and should be medically evaluated.

Sometimes a bulking agent or high-fibre preparation or colon stimulant preparation will be recommended. As a general rule, more significant degrees of constipation should be medically evaluated as significant constipation, particularly if associated with other symptoms, can indicate a number of disease states.

Obviously, diarrhoea, abnormal bowel actions (blood or mucus in the stool) and any degree of faecal incontinence are not part of normal ageing and should always be fully evaluated medically.

Sleep

This is a subject which has justifiably been given increasing attention in recent years. Many elderly people have difficulty with sleep and have abnormal sleep patterns and sometimes do not receive the best advice about this.

There are a few specific changes in sleep patterns that could be considered part of normal ageing. Older people tend not to sleep more than about 7–8 hours for a variety of reasons:

- their brains have become conditioned to about that length of sleep over many years
- older people tend to be a little stiffer in their joints and back and will often experience the desire to get up and move about after about that length of time in bed
- bladder (and bowel) capacity and function will often not permit longer periods of time without evacuation
- a pronounced degree of snoring is common in most adult males (and some females) and elderly males do not differ in this. However a change in the pattern of snoring may be significant.

Significant insomnia, frequent periods of early waking, the necessity to pass urine more than once or twice overnight, severe snoring and/or long periods of absence of respiration (apnoea), breathlessness, chest pains and other symptoms overnight should never be regarded as part of normal ageing. When any of these things occur they should be medically evaluated as they can be indicative of serious medical illnesses.

Similarly, excessive daytime sleepiness (somnolence) should not be regarded as a feature of normal ageing. However, if elderly parents rise relatively early and have an active morning, they may feel tired and benefit from a nap after lunch. If elderly parents are frequently falling asleep 'at the drop of a hat' during the day, this may be a symptom of obstructive sleep apnoea, or related to other medical factors such as the effects of medications. Such conditions require medical evaluation and intervention.

Many elderly people will be regular users of sleeping tablets (hypnotics) and may regard this as either normal for them or necessary for them to get to sleep. Hypnotics should generally only be prescribed for short-term insomnia in difficult circumstances (eg. acute hospital- isation, travel, bereavement reactions). After prolonged use elderly people can have features of pharmacological dependence on these agents. Once a person has become dependent, withdrawal has to be done slowly and with caution.

Elderly parents should be encouraged with good sleep habits through:

- avoidance of caffeine-containing drinks in the latter part of the day
- good bedtime habits (perhaps a warm milk drink)
- not becoming dependent on medications for sleeping.

Cardiovascular function

While a considerable number of cardiovascular disease states are age-related, normal ageing has few specific effects that should be detectable by adult children.

The physiological changes that accompany ageing, such as a decrease in elasticity of the peripheral arteries and slight slowing of the conduction system, are not of a nature that would be detectable by adult children. In the absence of specific disabilities or diseases, there are elderly people who regularly enjoy aerobic exercise such as walking, swimming or cycling significant distances.

Even though normal ageing is associated with a slight decline in cardiovascular endurance, this can be more than offset by the beneficial conditioning effects of regular aerobic exercise, to the extent that an elderly person with a regular exercise pattern may well be capable of more sustained aerobic exercise than someone who is many years younger!

The rapidity of cardiovascular reflexes slows slightly with normal ageing. Thus slight unsteadiness may occur with getting up from a chair or with first getting out of bed in the morning. Referred to as postural hypotension, this is a failure of the cardiovascular reflexes to compensate quickly enough for the change in posture after sitting or lying for a considerable period of time.

This phenomenon is not specific to ageing. The reaction can be exacerbated by certain blood pressure drugs.

However, it should be distinguished from more serious forms of collapse or near collapse where the person may be experiencing near collapse states with just standing or ordinary walking. Such symptoms can be indicative of significant malfunctioning of the heart's conducting system (first-degree or second-degree heart block) or valvular heart disease and, as such, are abnormal states that require investigation and the appropriate treatment.

Symptoms

Symptoms such as chest pains or tightness, palpitations, or significant breathlessness in the absence of significant exertion are indicative of cardiovascular disease and should never be attributed to 'just old age'. Similarly, cramps in the calves or buttocks with exertion or pains at night are a symptom of peripheral vascular disease. While this is partly an age-related condition, more significant risk factors are cigarette smoking, diabetes and high blood fats. Clearly, these symptoms require full evaluation and should never be dismissed as 'just old age'.

Joints, muscles and bones

There is a high degree of correlation between common perceptions of old age and changes in joints, muscles and bones. Despite this, however, the actual changes that are part of normal ageing as opposed to disease states, are fairly minimal.

Typically joints lose some of their laxity due to tissue changes and this is associated with a decreased range of movement of the order of 20 per cent or slightly more, compared to peak mobility earlier in life. However, such loss should not detract from most light forms of exercise.

Muscles usually lose between 20 and 30 per cent of their bulk compared to peak condition in the mid-thirties. There is good evidence that regular exercise slows decline and that even exercise programs instituted relatively late in life can reverse some of these changes and lead to improvement in muscle bulk and power.

Bones are well known to progressively lose their mineral density and mass with age. Like many other attributes associated with ageing, the end result will be dependent on the degree of a person's 'reserve' prior to the decline process. Gender is the major distinguishing factor when it comes to bone mass.

While the female and the male both lose significant bone mass with ageing, the male has a much greater bone mass and density to begin with. The female hormone oestrogen plays an important role in maintaining bone mass in the female and declines at menopause in the absence of hormone replacement therapy. The male hormone (testosterone) which also plays a role in bone mineralisation, does not have the same dramatic decline at a similar time of life.

Thus the only changes in joints that could be considered part of normal ageing could be mild stiffness of the joints in the mornings and after exercise, particularly exercise involving unaccustomed forms of exertion and lots of bending and stretching manoeuvres. Significant degrees of stiffness and pain that occur after more than the first ten minutes of the day should not be attributed just to ageing. Such symptoms, as well as others, such as swelling, redness, tenderness and deformity of joints are symptoms of a variety of rheumatological conditions which should be investigated and treated.

Only minimal muscle changes should be attributed to old age alone and these can be minimised with regular exercise. The most common form of thinner and weaker muscles is 'disuse atrophy' which can be prevented by regular exercise. The next most common is the local muscle loss that occurs in relation to any joint affected by an arthritic condition. Thus significant loss of muscle bulk and power is usually an abnormal state and should be investigated and treated.

Osteoporosis

Post-menopausal osteoporosis is by definition an age-related condition. The best documented risk factors for osteoporosis are:

• the post-menopausal state
• poor calcium and vitamin D dietary intake
• cigarette smoking
• a high salt diet and low exercise pattern in earlier life
• the consumption of some medications most notably cortisone derivatives.

Obviously the best preventative measures are the opposites of all these risk factors.

Fractures are a common sign of the onset of osteo-porosis. Thus any fracture that occurs with minimal trauma in an elderly parent should be regarded as due to osteoporosis unless proven otherwise. This has not been a perspective of health professionals until recently and you may need to advocate for your parents.

Water works — the urinary system

Again this is an area where strong cultural stereotypes exist, but where, in fact, some of the commonest abnormalities are manifestations of disease states rather than normal ageing.

In the male only the mildest of changes in the urinary pattern should be attributed to normal ageing. A significant degree of increased frequency of passing urine, the necessity to pass urine more than once overnight, a significant decrease in the urinary stream are, in fact, symptoms of bladder-neck obstruction generally due to enlargement of the prostate gland.

Prostate

Prostate enlargement, usually of a benign cause, is a classical age-related condition to the extent that its incidence has been estimated at nearly 100 per cent if a male reaches the age of one hundred. However it is a disease of ageing rather than part of ageing itself. When such symptoms develop in the aged, they should always be referred for medical assessment and treatment.

Incontinence

Urinary incontinence in either sex is not part of normal ageing and should always be seen as a symptom of some form of urinary system or related disease and thus requires optimal medical evaluation and treatment.

Not even in a female who has experienced multiple childbirth should the slightest degree of intermittent stress incontinence be regarded as within the limits of normal ageing. All urinary symptoms in a female should be regarded as abnormal and appropriately evaluated.

Skin

Despite the perception of substantial changes occurring in the skin with ageing, the changes that can be attributed to normal ageing are fairly limited.

With age, the skin has fewer fatty acids, less inherent moisture and it loses some of its elasticity. Ageing skin is thus susceptible to drying and care should be taken with soaps of all kinds. At best these are unnecessary and at worst they can produce excessive drying and irritation. The only other change that could be regarded as consistent with normal ageing is the appearance on the backs of the hands and forearms of purple blue spots known as 'senile purpura'. These are thought to be due to an increased fragility of the skin with ageing. However, more widespread bruising which occurs with minimal trauma should be brought to the attention of your parents' doctor.

In Australia, a large majority of our parents have been adversely affected by sun exposure to their skin. Thus, many of our parents technically have sun damaged skin, and so they exhibit a variety of lesions generally known as 'sunspots', and this needs to be distinguished from normal ageing. So, as well as considerable efforts to minimise further sun exposure in their old age, such spots should be monitored carefully for changes, and these should be the subject of specialist review and, in most cases, surgical excision for diagnostic and therapeutic reasons.

Conclusion

The general context of ageing and some of the major physical aspects of ageing have been reviewed. The limits of what can be attributed to normal ageing have been described and these descriptions should assist you with understanding what can, and, more importantly, what cannot be attributed to normal ageing of your older parents.

Poem

There is nothing wrong with me, I'm as healthy as I can be. I have arthritis in both my knees and when I talk I talk with a wheeze. My pulse is weak and my blood is thin, but I'm awfully well for the state I'm in.

Arch supports I have for my feet, or I wouldn't be able to walk up the street. Sleep is denied me night after night, but every morning I find I'm alright. My memories fading, my heads in a spin, but I'm awfully well for the shape I'm in.

The moral is this as my tale I unfold, that for you and me who are getting old, it's better to say 'I'm fine' with a grin than to let folks know the shape we're in.

How do I know my health is spent? Well my 'Get up and go' has got up and went! But I don't really mind when I think with a grin of all the grand places my 'Get up' has been.

Old age is golden I've heard it said but sometimes I wonder as I get into bed. With my ears in the drawer and my teeth in a cup, my eyes on the table till I wake up. Ere sleep overtakes me I say to myself 'is there anything else I can lay on the shelf?'

When I was young my slippers were red and I could kick up my heels right up to my head. When I was older my slippers were blue but I could still dance the whole night through. Now I am old my slippers are black, I walk to the store and I puff my way back.

I get up each morning and dust-off my wits then pick up the paper and read the Obits. If my name is still missing I know I'm not dead so I have a good breakfast and go back to bed.

Author unknown

4 One day we might have to look after them but in the meantime

Prevention — how you can help your parents to stay as independent as possible

You might have agreed that, one day, you will help to look after your parents. But, in the meantime, there are a lot of simple preventative measures that can help older people retain their independence and avoid injury — therefore putting off that day as long as possible!

Fit, well and independent older people can change dramatically with a sudden serious illness or a fall. Your parents may believe that they are health and safety conscious — but are they?

Here are some handy home hints about how to help your parents avoid accidents and maintain as much of their physical strength as possible.

Safety first — how to avoid falls

Falls are a major cause of injury in older people. Statistics show that the majority of falls of older people resulting in serious injury, occur in and around the home. Because older people's bones are more frail, they can easily break hip bones, knees, arms and wrists, meaning they suddenly require a lot of help to undertake everyday tasks such as cooking or bathing. Even after lengthy rehabilitation, your parents may be unable to resume some self-care tasks that they once did with ease.

Because of this there are 'falls prevention' programs funded by the Commonwealth Government which specifically aim to reduce falls amongst older people. Falls prevention advisers, occupational therapists or physiotherapists can visit older people at home and advise them about reducing the risk of falls around the home.

Story

*I*IMAGINE YOU WOULD HAVE *heard about mum's 'fall' by now but in case you haven't, she tripped on a bit of wood in the dark and twisted one knee and bruised the other. The next day, after much pain and hesitation, and after spending the night in the chair, she agreed to call an ambulance to take her to hospital. After a day in casualty on a trolley, the verdict is that she has torn the medial ligament in one leg and badly bruised the other. The hospital plastered it up and sent her home with a pair of crutches, but she was pretty much immobile and couldn't really walk or move around.*

We contacted the local community health centre and explained the situation and they sent an occupational therapist and a physiotherapist around that afternoon. They organised some temporary aids for showering and the bathroom, raised her bed to make it easier to get in and out of, and provided a special chair for her. The local meals service is providing meals-on-wheels a couple of days a week and the rest of us are providing some meals whenever we can. The doctor said she will be out of action for at least four weeks but probably quite a bit longer. At least she is comfortable now, getting physio, on the road to recovery and back doing her crosswords.

There are plenty of things to do to help your older parents to remain 'going' concerns (and avoid falling). Start by suggesting or encouraging them to:

- look after and maintain their feet, including using professional treatments by a podiatrist
- maintain good balance — either by exercising to keep their strength and/or handy rails and supports, such as a walking stick or frame which has been measured specifically for them by a physiotherapist or other health professional (avoid just using grandpa's old stick!)
- take several small steps to turn around instead of swivelling around quickly
- buy good quality and well fitting shoes with broad flattish non-slip (rubber not leather) heels. This means those old gardening shoes too — out with them if they are down at heel.
- upgrade their eye glasses regularly, including sunglasses for out of doors
- have good lighting around the house and use 100 watt bulbs — seeing is not tripping!
- allow time for their eyes to adjust to different lighting levels before walking
- treat or replace slippery or uneven surfaces, like mossy paths, shiny brick paving, broken concrete or sloping areas with a gravel surface
- avoid walking on wet or damp floors, especially when you have just washed them
- remove debris, fallen leaves and slime from paths and driveways
- repair and eliminate bumps and cracks in pathways in the yard, especially around the clothes line
- walk around rather than across uneven surfaces
- mark the edges of steps around the home by painting a white strip along the edge
- slow down when approaching steps or curbs
- have rails installed next to steps and use them every time

- check if medication has a side effect of making them dizzy
- check medication for side effects when taken with alcohol
- use bathroom safety aids such as rails and rubber mats to reduce the possibility of slipping
- check floor coverings — get rid of rugs that slide on floors or turn up at the corners
- consider replacing steps with ramps or adding hand rails for extra stability and support
- report to your parents' local government body any fall hazards in their neighbourhood and be insistent that these hazards be rectified
- get rid of that 'spaghetti' mass of electrical cords zigzagging across the floor
- clear a pathway from the bed to the toilet — for those quick night trips!
- consider sitting down to put on knickers or underdaks. Leaping into these garments is fraught with danger in that hazardous room in the house — the bathroom.

Fear of falling

For older people, even the fear of falling can lead to not going out or exercising. In turn, this can lead to weakness of muscles, poorer balance, reduced ability of muscles and bones to support the person and reduction in the intake of calcium due to being indoors most of the time. So check out all the above, then encourage your parents to keep doing things in and outside the house.

Many older people are really worried about falling and not being found for some days. You need to discuss this with your parents. Having a plan of action worked out for them in advance is useful as it can be hard to think clearly at the time of an accident. They can try simple things like:
- crawling to a sturdy piece of furniture and pulling themselves up

- crawling to a warm spot and trying to get up later when they feel better
- having telephones placed on low rather than high tables, shelves or wall mountings
- seeing if they can actually get up off the floor by themselves. If not, a physiotherapist could teach them how to get up safely.
- wearing a personal alarm to activate help, if needed.

Exercise — what is it and how much is enough?

Nobody is too old for exercise — it just has to be geared to the person's ability at the time. In fact, people really cannot afford NOT to exercise. The preventative value of exercise is well recognised in regard to osteoporosis — a common problem for older women involving a loss of bone density.

Exercise will increase the heart rate, build up heart muscle and increase the oxygen supply to the body. Exercise also helps prevent stiffness, yet so many people do not exercise because they are stiff. Exercise can also improve sleep and promotes a general feeling of well-being.

Some form of gentle exercise every day is ideal, unless your parents are unwell. To gain the most benefit, your parents should build up to some level of 'puff', but not so much that they could not talk at the same time as exercising. If not used to exercise, they should start with a very short routine and gradually increase the time spent on it. Each bout of exercise should start slowly in order to 'warm up' and finish with a period of decreasing effort in order to 'cool down'.

Rather than try to get your parents to embrace a new exercise routine that you enjoy, take into account the well-documented fact that people continue to like doing things they have always liked doing, even if it is in a reduced or modified way. So, identify your parents' long-standing interests, perhaps walking, swimming, gardening, cooking or bird-watching, and work out how they can be helped to still follow these interests in some way.

Of course, if your parents have always been ones for doing something new, having something different to talk about, then they would most likely love to hear your ideas about a new recreation for them. Tai chi is a wonderful form of exercise that many older people take up. Yoga can be beneficial. Local papers carry advertisements about courses which are often run by University of the Third Age (U3A), neighbourhood houses or Community Health Services.

Before starting any new form of activity, it is best for your parents to have an overall check by their doctor to discuss the exercise they are planning to do. The doctor may suggest your parents be guided by a physiotherapist before commencing an exercise routine, if they have some problems that could be aggravated by exercise.

Walking

Walking around the house, around the garden, up the street, short slow walks and long purposeful walks are all very good weight-bearing exercise and are easy to do. While it is good to move often-used items to cupboards and places that are easily reached, it is not a good policy to set your parents up with everything in easy reach of their armchair, unless they really cannot walk.

Groups for walking and gentle exercise for older people are provided at the local level by local government recreation services, community health centres, self-help groups, U3A, neighbourhood houses and a host of other organisations. Private enterprise walking groups also provide great encouragement through group partici-pation. Walking groups called 'Neighbourhood Walk 'n' Talk Program' are established in most areas across Australia.

Swimming

Swimming is a great exercise, because it is not too hard on older bodies, with the buoyancy helping movement and easing stiff joints. Many older people find the water is too cold in the sea or regular swimming pools, even if heated. Hydrotherapy pools are heated to a higher level which may be uncomfortable for swimming but is gorgeous for exercising in the water. Contact your parents' local government or shire office to find out if there is a pool near their home. Hydrotherapy pools may be located at health centres, rehabilitation centres and public swimming pools, and there are also private hydrotherapy pools. Charges differ widely for there are many ways to be involved, including being:

- a private or public patient of a physiotherapist who has time allotted for individual or group sessions at a public, community centre or private hydrotherapy pool
- an ex-patient of a rehabilitation service and being included in a self-help group at a public, community centre or private pool
- an individual resident using the local public hydro-therapy pool for exercise
- a person who has gained access to a hydrotherapy pool at a community health centre for self-help groups.

Gyms

Many private enterprise gymnasiums and health clubs give special rates and often waive joining fees for older people. Gyms usually require a medical clearance from your doctor that it is safe for you to undertake a certain level of exercise, and obtaining this is wise. If this idea appeals to your parents they will often not be the only older people there. Acceptance by 'the bronzed and beautiful' is usually forthcoming because they hope they will still be attending when they are 'that old'.

Do-it-yourself (DIY) injuries

Your parents may be among the many people who have saved up jobs around the house to keep them busy in their retirement. On the one hand, this can be very satisfying, add value to a property and provide the opportunity to be productively occupied. However, there is a hazard if your parents are not used to undertaking such manual tasks and will be using unfamiliar tools. The Victorian Injury Surveillance System, which keeps the most detailed injury statistics in Australia, found the number of hospital admissions as a result of DIY injuries (such as falls from ladders or injuries from power tools) have increased significantly over the past ten years. Almost 40 per cent of DIY injuries occurred in people aged between 50 and 69.

While not wishing to discourage your parents' DIY projects, it is probably worth mentioning that these jobs often look much easier on the garden and home improvement programs presented on television than they turn out to be when an amateur gets started. If your parents are keen to get on with DIY projects, at least check out the ladder and their balance!

Of course, if an accident does happen, for whatever reason, be sure to help maintain the usual interests or activities they pursued prior to the accident throughout their recovery. This can be done by keeping them up to date with news from their bowling, golf or social club, and engaging them in discussion of the sport or interest in the wider community, competitions, issues and the like. Keep their acquaintances informed about their progress to pave the way for their return to the club or activity, even if it has to be in a modified way. Be creative in your ideas about how to do this, like getting your parent to write a few lines for the club newsletter or notice board. Do not overlook the role a computer can play in keeping your parent occupied while rehabilitating.

─────────── *Story* ───────────

*J*ACK'S GOLFING COMPANIONS WERE *pleased to get his message that although he had severely injured his leg in a fall (having slipped on gum leaves while walking the dog), he was determined to return to golf in the next few months. He warned them not to write him off just yet even if he is 82. He advised that he was still playing and actually improving his game — strategically, that is. The family had hired him a computer for three months while he was recovering and he was playing golf on the computer. He told them the game is just as interesting and every bit as frustrating on the screen as it is on the course. But still he's doing all his rehabilitation exercises because he wants to get back on the course proper — for the grass and the friends.*

Silver web-surfers (computer users)

Do not overlook the asset a computer and the internet can be to an older person. Enabling an older person to use a computer opens up many opportunities. For a start, it includes them in goings-on of this era. Imagine if, when television came in, you were merely by-passed and never learned how to use one, never owned one, never had access to one. Further, imagine that you had to listen to family and others talk about all the things they enjoyed on television, while yourself being 'the dummy' who knew nothing about the set or what they were talking about. One way to help convince your parents they are old and 'past it' is to leave them out of things. Just as the television joined record players, the radio, the piano, card and board games, holiday slides and home movies as part of home entertainment, so too can computers.

Among the opportunities that computer skills provide for older people are:

- reducing isolation and loneliness
- being an 'inie' not an 'outie'
- feeling satisfaction with skills gained

- experiencing frustration — adds to the interest of the day
- bridging the inter-generational gap — including rapport with grandchildren
- providing banking and shopping facilities via the internet
- increasing communication with others by sharing tidbits of information via the internet
- giving them something to talk about
- opening up access to information and games.

Even if providing a computer for your parent is not an option, do encourage them to learn to operate one. Many public libraries across the country have computer classes for older people, as do neighbourhood houses, University of the Third Age, volunteer organisations and other providers of education. Once your parent has learned to use a computer then there are a variety of places they can book time to use them, including local public libraries, some senior citizens clubs and cafes.

Eating

Older people often say that once you turn 80 everyone decides to tell you what to eat, how to live, what to do. It seems that having got to 80 they may have a fair idea. Rather than encouraging you to become a 'nag', it is hoped this book will guide you in what to look for and alternatives to consider if you notice that your parents are changing significantly. Sudden weight gain or loss, or significant mood, behaviour or attitude changes should alert you to consider whether your parents are eating wisely and whether there is some health or social problem worrying them.

Don't rely on the old myths such as 'starve a fever, feed a cold' — what if they have a feverish cold? Your parents' doctor will be a better source of information as will the dietitian at a community health centre. The National

Health and Medical Research Council has produced a wonderful full-colour booklet with recipes, advice about nutritious food, food preparation and storage to prevent food poisoning, how to choose foods low in salt, and the most easily absorbed sources of calcium in food. Ring the Department of Health and Aged Care, or its equivalent in your state, to see where you can obtain a copy. (See pages 157–60.)

Regardless of all the good information available, myths persist in regard to older people and food. Some common beliefs are:

- old people do not need to eat much
- getting thin and frail is natural for the aged
- if you are overweight there is nothing you can do about it.

Eating enough is not about volume, but about nutritional value of what your parents eat. A dietitian can advise and encourage your parents to eat appropriately for them.

Poor nutrition in the elderly can lead to:

- increased risk of falls
- increased risk of infections
- poor wound recovery
- poor recovery from illness or surgery
- increased frailty.

All these in turn have the potential to reduce your parents' quality of life and even to affect they way they will live the rest of their lives — whether they will be on their feet or chair-bound or bed-bound.

If your parents are just a little overweight, it is not necessarily a bad thing, unless it is a sudden change — in which case they should see their doctor about it. Being slightly overweight in older people does, in fact, provide some protection because they have some reserves to fall back on if they become stressed or ill. It even offers some cushioning factor if they fall.

Nevertheless, if your parents are moderately or very overweight they will be feeling the stress on their bodies. For older people, being overweight can aggravate back and knee problems, place increased stress upon joints, and lead to increased tiredness and reduced activity. However, it is not helpful for them to just diet to try to reduce weight — maintaining moderate food intake (to avoid more weight gain) and increasing movement and exercise is the best approach.

Drinking

Drinking adequate amounts of fluid is just as important for your parents as eating adequate amounts of food. Because many older people are worried or frustrated and annoyed by the constant need to go to the toilet to urinate, they decide to cut back on fluids. The way to check if someone is having enough fluids is that, except for first thing in the morning, their urine should be an almost clear colour. You can hardly check this, but you could talk to your parents about it and interest them in checking. Producing dark yellow urine is a sign of inadequate fluid intake, and can lead to dehydration, kidney problems, urinary tract infections or kidney stones and constipation. Many foods such as soup, jellies, ice-cream, custards and the like are also a good source of fluid if your parents cannot be persuaded to drink more.

Alcohol

As people age, the amount of alcohol that is safe for them to drink decreases. As with younger people, the safe amount for an older woman is less than for an older man. Many people benefit greatly from the added enjoyment of a drink or two with a meal. It can also stimulate appetite and small amounts may even provide some protection against heart disease. Just as with driving a car, the measure of what is enough is often spoken of in terms of 'standard drinks' and no more than two a day is suggested for older people. A standard drink is:

- a glass of wine
- a middie of beer (285 mls)
- a schooner of low-alcohol beer (570 mls)
- a nip of spirits.

You may have a problem if your parents consume, or perhaps have always consumed, too much alcohol. It may not be compatible with your parents' medication, and may make them more prone to falls. Often an older person's health can improve quite dramatically if they reduce their alcohol intake.

Smoking

What can be said? Research has clearly demonstrated the health risks associated with smoking, not only for the actual person smoking, but also for others in the same room or close by. Some home help and home visiting health professionals will insist on a smoke-free environment while they are working. If your parents do smoke, remind them that they will be doing everyone a big favour by cutting down or quitting.

Skin

Skin, it keeps your insides in, so look after it! In older people skin can become dry and fragile, and slow to heal from surface breaks and knocks which often result in ulcers. Medications can have side effects which cause itchy rashes. Scratching leads to breaks in the surface of the skin. The earlier your parents start to look after their skin using moisturiser, the better. Dads may be more difficult to get cooperation from on this one. These days, the 'slip, slop, slap' message is well promoted, and you should make sure that your parents have plenty of sunscreen too. Encourage them to keep a 'map' of skin spots and consult their doctor for referral to a skin specialist for any spots that are changing or may indicate a skin cancer.

Teeth

Many older people may have poorly fitting dentures, heat and cold sensitive (touchy) teeth, or mouth ulcers. All these conditions certainly diminish the enjoyment of eating and can lead to a lack of confidence. Encourage your parents to have at least an annual check up by their dentist. Most publicly funded dental services have waiting lists but if an elderly person has tooth pain, an appointment is usually given fairly quickly.

Hygiene

Many people worry that their parents will become grubby old people. Some do; why does this happen? Firstly the senses of smell and eyesight deteriorate with age. Also, the effort to wash yourself, your clothes and house can be much greater, and if you are stuck alone in the house all day, who cares? Being neat and clean has to do with self-esteem and opportunity, so deriding the person won't help. It is much better to do something practical. Assistance with showering and hair washing — called 'personal care' — can be provided by support services.

House-cleaning

Don't assume your parents' house is dirty just because it is not as clean as yours. Help with keeping the house clean is often the first type of assistance your parents will consider — especially the vacuum cleaning and cleaning the bath and shower, as these jobs are so hard on the back. Chapter 6 details services that help older people with the house-work.

It is a good idea to get your parents to start accepting

help with household jobs if their lifelong habit has been to do everything for themselves. There are two difficult tasks that are not generally, or regularly, covered by support services. These two tasks cause worry and concern to older people trying to maintain themselves in their own homes. They are the heavy gardening and the lawns, and cleaning the windows inside and out.

Before your parents are frail, it can be a good opportunity to rally extended family support by getting your parents to organise someone to regularly do these tasks for them and have the family pick up the bill. It can be a birthday or Christmas present from the whole family. It is an example of how they can retain control over their household, because they choose the person and outline the tasks to be done, while accepting assistance from both the worker and their family.

Health screenings

There are a number of health screening programs that are available to older people. These include screening programs for cancer (such as smear tests and mammograms for women, and prostrate checks for men) as well as immunisation (against winter colds and respiratory problems) and general health assessment and screening programs. Your parents' local doctor can advise on these.

Sexuality and intimacy

If your own sex life is almost non-existent, don't assume it is the same for your parents! They may be less stressed and have more time than you do. They may even have a better relationship than you do with your partner. It is best to assume that your parents still enjoy intimacy, affection and a physical aspect to their relationship. This way you will be sensitive to their need for privacy and they will appreciate the respect.

Older minds

Given that losses are a significant part of the lives of most older people, it is not surprising that they can feel depressed. Spare a thought for the losses your parents may have suffered, perhaps:

- the death of partner, friends, children
- the loss of meaningful occupation of time, physical or mental function and along with that the loss of self-identity, power, position and feeling needed
- the loss of neighbourhood, community connections
- the loss of self-reliance
- reduced financial resources.

For 'down in the dumps', sadness, continual flat and uninterested feelings that we all experience at times, help your parents to put into practice the things they have always done to lift their spirits. For severe and continuing depression, encourage your parents to consult their doctor.

Having a positive outlook is, of course, a great asset. Do not expect your parents to develop one if they have not had this orientation all their lives. Even if they have been a positive outgoing person, ageing may change them. Being positive can wear thin for people if they do not see much to be positive about. Perhaps you can help revive a positive outlook by providing some positive experiences for them.

Always try to display a positive attitude towards your parents. If the phrase 'silly old buggers' springs to mind when you think of your parents, change your tune, before they start fulfilling your expectations. For example, if your older parent does fall off a ladder and break a leg at 80 plus, avoid saying to hospital staff or other people that the 'silly old bugger' fell off a ladder. A positive introduction, which may illicit much better treatment, would be 'My father is a wonderful independent man. He was cleaning out the gutters when he fell.'

Feeling safe

It is realistic for older people to feel vulnerable. The neglected garden, the rails at the steps or a run-down building often indicate a frail older household. By the same token, things can be done to minimise vulnerability. Helpful neighbours are invaluable. Simple signs, like a blind up by 10 am, can be worked out between older people and their neighbours to show that all is well or that help is needed.

Neighbourhood Watch Programs, which operate throughout Australia, have an emphasis on watching out for neighbours' property, but will also add to your parents' feeling of security.

Victoria Police Confident Living Program is designed to encourage older people to feel safe at home, when driving, on public transport and in the community. Police will talk to groups of older people and tell them the things they can do to feel and be safe. In New South Wales similar services are available through Community Safety Liaison Officers at police area headquarters. Check with police headquarters in your state for details.

Staying alert

Don't let your parents just settle down to be old. Play your part in helping them keep alert by engaging them in conversations. Try to stimulate their thinking. Tell them family news.

If phone calls become a duty and you let your mind freewheel while they moan on about their lot, change the subject, engage them, challenge them. Encourage them to maintain a lively interest in the things which have held their interest in the past. If your parents settle down to old age at 65 plus, you may have to deal with this for the next twenty years!

Don't talk your parents into being old/confused

Little slips of memory are not dementia. Dementia is a condition where there is a general loss of intellectual ability which occurs through physical changes in the brain. Doctors diagnose dementia using a combination of methods including observing behaviour, considering the person's ability to undertake everyday tasks, and physiological testing such as blood tests and CAT scans. Don't assume your parents have dementia until they have been properly assessed by medical specialists, as there may be other causes of their problems. Unfortunately the terms 'dementia', 'short-term memory loss' and 'Alzheimer's disease' have become part of a culture of jokes — in part, people whistling to keep up their courage — but these conditions are no laughing matter.

Don't 'harp' on the times your parents have forgotten something. We all forget things from time to time — the balance is in knowing when to be worried about it, whether it is affecting the older person's independence, and when professional help might be needed. There are plenty of strategies older people use to compensate for their forgetfulness, and these can work very well and to their satisfaction.

Story
---

*T*HE ASSESSMENT OFFICER AT *the local government authority received a phone call requesting that someone visit an elderly aunt (May) and assess her for home help services. The assessor obtained May's details and told the niece she would contact May to arrange a time to visit her. The niece went on to say that it would be impossible to make an arrangement with May as she would never remember what it was about, what day or time, or who was coming. The assessor said that she would ring May and if unable to make the arrangement directly with her would ring the niece and ask her to assist in getting the visit time arranged. The niece was* *angry about the delay, assuring the assessor that the phone call to the aunt would be upsetting and confusing for the 85-year-old lady suffering from Alzheimer's disease. The assessor really wanted to talk directly to the aunt to see if she wanted the niece to be present for the visit, but was persuaded, against her better judgement, to let the niece make the arrangement for the visit.*

When the assessor visited May, the niece was present. May was a small, thin but spritely lady, in a neat clean house, who was understandably very cross. She did not want anyone to do her housework for her. 'I need something to do all day,' she said. The assessor told her that if she did not want the help, of course, she did not have to accept it, but would she like to hear what was available. May was surprised and said 'I thought I would not have any choice. I thought you would believe I cannot manage.' The niece wanted her aunt to accept help and continue to manage at home. She insisted, 'Auntie May, you just cannot manage. You have Alzheimer's disease, you cannot remember our phone numbers, you make lists of things to do each day, your calendar is written all over with notes about what you are supposed to be doing, you have even mislaid your passport'.

'Yes,' said May, 'but I found it in time to complete my booking to go to New Zealand next month'.

Sounds like May had lots of strategies to help her remember things and was really doing quite well. And of course the housework help, a limited resource, was not forced on May.

Passing time

Once work and family-rearing have ceased, a person needs to pass time in a way that is meaningful to them. For some people this means getting through the day without any hassles. For others it means getting something done. Don't bombard your parents with suggestions of what you think they should be doing, based on what other lively old people you know are doing. Just find out what they want to do and see if you can facilitate their doing it. Remember, reduced financial resources can separate people from their interests. Hobbies or entertainment cost money. Opportunities for meaningful gifts exist in these areas.

Dealing with loneliness

There is an amazing range of activities provided at local levels for older people. Your local government, community health centre or local newspaper are good places to start seeing what's on. People may seem lonely to you because they are on their own, but as you know we can be lonely when we are with people with whom we have nothing in common. We can also be alone but not in the least lonely. So listen to your parents if they say they are lonely, then work out with them what options they have to change this situation.

As with people of all ages, older people cannot be seen as a homogeneous group with similar views or interests. As individuals, your parents may differ enormously from each other and from other older people in the amount of company or mental stimulation they need. Work with older people over the years indicates that some people want more and more opportunities to go out with a group, day trips, the cinema, meals, concerts and the like. Others have very firmly stated that while they were 'bored stiff' at home they wouldn't be seen 'dead' with one of those rowdy groups of old people.

Are my parents a menace on the road?

If your parents are used to driving their own car, they are likely to dread the day when their 'licence is taken away'. The loss of independence of movement will be enormous. You may be concerned about your parents' driving skills but do not want to be the 'bad guy' who tells them it is time to stop driving. Well, don't let it be you — perhaps the older person's doctor can assess and advise them. There are some positive actions to take that may result in your parents becoming better older drivers, or else coming to the decision to stop driving themselves.

The Royal Auto Club, or its equivalent in each state, provides a driver assessment service. For a moderate fee they will assess your parents' driving skills and indicate the areas in which they exhibit driving faults and how they could improve their driving skills. There are no repercussions in regard to the driver's licence. The service provides advice for which you pay. The wise thing to do is heed the advice.

'Wiser Drivers' courses also exist in some states. These courses voluntarily bring older drivers together with a trained facilitator to discuss the issues and practices of their driving. The group helps each participant to come to their own decision about whether they should still be driving. No compulsion exists to take advice from the group.

Rehabilitation centres and some hospitals also provide driver assessments. The professionals making these assessments do have the right to advise authorities that a licence should be cancelled or not renewed.

If your parents are no longer able to drive, it can be helpful to set out for them on paper the cost of owning and running their car. Without the car they would have 'x' amount of dollars to spend on taxis each week. Once again, it could be an opportunity to marshal family resources and instead of giving your parents a 'toe cover' for Christmas, provide them with a cab charge card — and a limit!

Taxis

If your parents have physical or mental impairments which make it difficult for them to use public transport, they can obtain an application form and apply for a half-price taxi concession. Their doctor can supply the form and will need to complete the portion of the application concerning their health.

Many older people have grown up in a culture where using a taxi was an extravagance only to be contemplated in dire emergencies. Even though they have the financial resources to pay for a taxi, they still exhibit great reluctance to do so. Fear is often a reason: fear the driver will be late, won't find the house, will get a better fare and won't come at all, will overcharge them, will know that they live alone, will drive off before they get to the door. Heard it all yourself?

Taxi companies are aware of these concerns and over the years have made some attempts to dispel these fears. Booking has been simplified. The preferred taxi company number can be entered into your parents' phone and their full details will be in front of the dispatcher instantly. Your parents do not need to say anything. No need to explain, 'It's the house on the corner with the door in the side street'. Pertinent details are pre-registered. Your parents just ring and start heading for the front door.

Some companies have specially vetted drivers who are assigned the jobs for older passengers. Some older people even have their own methods for getting their preferred driver in a particular taxi company. Other older people who use taxis are great sources of information as to how to get the best service.

Be supportive if your parents have to give up driving. To many people, the car is an extension of themselves, their power and image. Just put yourself in their shoes for a moment — and be kind about it.

Practical considerations

Have your parents made wills?

Have each of your parents made a will? If so, is it still appropriate? Making a will is really the only way a person can be sure that assets are distributed according to their wishes. Anyone can write out the will. It can be hand-written, typewritten or printed. A will must be signed by the person making the will and witnessed by two other people. Usually any person being left something in the will should not witness it.

The wording of the will is important because it ensures that the intentions of the person making it are clear. For this reason, it is a good idea to use a solicitor. A solicitor will charge a fee for drawing up the will. Shop around and ask what the charge will be. Some solicitors make wills in return for a donation to a charity they nominate. The Law Institute in your state can provide a list of names of solicitors who do this voluntary work. Community legal services and some charities may also be able give to you the names of solicitors who charge moderate fees for making wills.

A will can be drawn up free of charge by the Public Trustee or a private trustee company. However, the catch here is that they require to be named as executor of the will, which gives them the right to charge a commission for administering the estate. But a will should in any case name an executor or executors of the will. The executor's job is, among other duties, to see that the directions in the will are carried out. There are quite a few jobs for the executor to do, and if you do not wish to ask a family member or a friend, then you have the option of the Public Trustee or a trustee company to act as executor.

You may not feel like broaching the subject of making a will with your parents. If a person dies without leaving a will (dies intestate), their property is distributed to their next-of-kin according to a formula set out in the Administration and Probate Act. It does not just go into government coffers! However, if someone dies without leaving a will, all close relatives may need to be found. This may be complex, time consuming and expensive.

Have your parents given someone power of attorney?

There are different reasons for giving someone power of attorney, and thus, there are different types of power of attorney. In giving someone power of attorney, you are the donor of the power and this means you authorise them to act on your behalf. So you need to choose someone, or more than one person, you trust to be your attorney. Obviously, great care must be exercised when choosing an attorney. The attorney should keep the original document. A copy should be given to any alternative attorney and the donor should keep a copy.

A general power of attorney authorises the attorney to do, on the donor's behalf, anything which the attorney can lawfully be authorised to do. It can be stipulated to come into operation if the donor becomes ill. However, the general power of attorney is no longer valid if the donor becomes incapable of managing his or her affairs. While of sound mind, the donor can always revoke (cancel) this power of attorney.

The two most important powers of attorney for older people are an 'enduring power of attorney' and an 'enduring power of attorney: medical treatment' (the title may vary from state to state). Both these documents have to be drawn up in a special way and witnessed by two people. People would be well advised to engage a solicitor to do this for them.

An enduring power of attorney will cater for a wider set of circumstances, including the situation where the donor becomes incapable of managing his or her affairs. It can be arranged that the power operates only from that time.

An enduring power of attorney (medical treatment), allows the attorney, or alternate, to make decisions about medical treatment on your behalf when you are unable to do so. Medical treatment means an operation, the giving of medicine or drugs or any other medical procedure, but it does not include treatment which would relieve pain, suffering and discomfort or the provision of food and water.

A specific power of attorney can be given for a specific purpose, say to sell a certain property, or for a specific period of time, such as while you are overseas or on holiday.

If it is given voluntarily, a power of attorney can be cancelled at any time by the donor. However, if the donor becomes 'incapable', an enduring power of attorney can only be cancelled when the attorney, the Public Trustee or a person who has a special interest in the affairs of the donor applies to the Supreme Court to have the power revoked. There are also 'irrevocable powers of attorney', which are usually given for some consideration (such as for money or something of value), to allow the attorney to control some asset given as a security.

The issue of your older parents giving someone power of attorney is raised to encourage thought about this matter. The choice of the appropriate power of attorney can be a complicated matter and it is wise to discuss it with a solicitor you feel comfortable with and who understands your older parents' needs.

Important documents/papers

The best laid plans can go astray if the documents to support them cannot be easily located when needed. Your parents should keep all important documents together in a safe place, and tell several family members where they are being kept. Such documents may include:

- their wills
- birth and marriage certificates
- death certificates of any children who have died
- deed polls (name change documents)
- divorce decrees
- house title
- share certificates
- copies of powers of attorney
- funeral instructions and any prepaid funeral documents
- life and property insurance policies
- health fund details
- documents detailing any debts, loans or other arrangement effecting their assets
- mortgages
- partnerships
- details of jointly owned properties or items.

Keeping up appearances

The issue of older people concealing information or their true situation must be raised. If you make a ritual of calling to see your parents the same day of the week for the same sort of activity, say Sunday for morning tea, the chances are that no matter how poorly they are managing to get their food during the week, everything will look fine when you call on Sunday.

Maybe they want to present well so you won't worry. Maybe they enjoy your visit so much, they can make the effort and get a cup of tea and a biscuit together. Maybe they are financially stretched but put on a good show, with plenty of food when you call, but have very little the rest of the week. Proud older people are very good at keeping up appearances and not so long ago it was often an important family 'rule'. Just be aware of this concealment as it is a very common strategy for appearing to cope.

--- Story ---

*A*FTER DAD DIED, WE *were not so worried about how Mum would manage physically because she seemed to run the house like clockwork and she was getting Home Care from the local council. But we knew she would miss Dad terribly. They had been married for over sixty years. As they had been loving and supportive of each other, the family thought that loneliness, attending to the bills and managing money would be the big obstacles for Mum. To help with the mail and finances, I used to go over every Sunday (I had a full-time job, so mid-week was out). While there, I also gave a hand in the garden as Mum was a great gardener all her life and she missed Dad's help with the work.*

Whenever I called there was the freshly starched white embroidered cloth, posy of flowers, tasty biscuits and a cup of tea in her finest china. The house was neat and very clean as usual. We discussed the recipes she had tried during the week. Although I am no cook, she certainly was a very good cook and I was happy to hear all about the meals she was preparing.

'Gosh,' I thought, 'she is just doing so well'. Little did I know, until the local Home Care service advised me, that my mother was not coping at all. The supervisor suggested that I call over unexpectedly. Well, what a change! The house was in darkness at 6.30 pm in winter and not a meal in sight. She had forgotten how to put on the heater and the television and there was very little food in the fridge. This scene bore no relationship to the bright Sunday afternoon presentation.

I was grateful that the home carer was interested enough about Mum to report her concerns to her supervisor, and even more grateful that the supervisor contacted me. They really do that bit more than just clean the house.

Dealing with our society and its ageist attitudes

It is not until you begin to be classed as 'old' yourself that you really experience just how rampant ageism is in our society. Remember, most older people want to keep growing old as the alternative is not very appealing!

Story

A TECHNICIAN CALLING TO install another phone line to our home said, 'I can't understand you old people. How could you possibly need all these phones and two lines to the house as well?' In our home we do have five phone hand-sets, two mobiles, and two computers with email and internet. We are old but both still working as well as writing. So 'on your bike'!

Story

RECENTLY WHEN I WAS leaving a shop, the alarm was activated. A friendly shop assistant came up and said 'I can't understand how this has happened. They sometimes go off if a person has a mobile — but you wouldn't have one.' Wot, too bloody old! I did have one, in my bag, not grafted to my ear.

So spare a thought for your parents as they get older. No doubt they are having these brushes with the ageist society as well.

At the same time it may be worth checking out your own home and yourself in regard to the health and safety issues mentioned here. After all, we are all headed in the same direction!

5   Who's that and what do they do?

Simple descriptions of the role of different health professionals including some you may never have heard of

I HAVE A LIST OF QUESTIONS TO ASK YOU REGARDING MY ELDERLY PARENTS! ... FIRSTLY, DO YOU HAVE ENOUGH DRUGS TO HELP GET US THROUGH THEIR LAST YEARS?

GOLDING

Over the coming years you and your parents will probably come into contact with a wide range of medical and allied health professionals. This chapter explains the roles and responsibilities of these people, how you should expect them to communicate and work as a team, and how they can benefit your parents and you.

How can a general practitioner help older people?

Most older people do have a general practitioner or doctor whom they visit. In fact, many older people will have been consulting the same doctor for years. This is often a good thing because it means the doctor has a great deal of knowledge about your parents, their family and their medical history, but it can also be a disadvantage. Sometimes, too much trust and belief can be placed in a doctor simply because 'He has been seeing us for years; we always go to him'. It is surprising how useful a second opinion can be, and how sometimes a different doctor with a different approach may get better results or provide new and helpful information.

Encourage your older parents to attend a doctor they are happy and comfortable with, one who is happy to discuss their plans for ageing generally, not just the particular medical issue at hand. It is a good idea for a family member to go with the older person to the doctor to have another set of ears, as the older person may not hear properly or may get confused. It is also a good idea to have prepared a list of questions to ask the doctor and to note the answers. Perhaps your parents will agree to a joint consultation with you and their doctor about their overall health and their future plans, with a view to the doctor commenting on their chances of living in the way they want to and predicting what sort of help may be needed. Your parents may think this is too intrusive. If so, at least register your name and contact details with their doctor in writing. Professional ethics will ensure the doctor does not tell you anything your parents do not wish you to know. But be sure the doctor knows you are around and interested.

If your parents are not comfortable or satisfied with their doctor, then, as with any service provider, shop around. Help your parents to find a doctor they feel understands their situation and in whom they have confidence. The doctor can be the critical component in managing your parents' health and well-being.

The Commonwealth Government has recently introduced a new Medicare item for people aged over 75 years. This enables doctors to do detailed and comprehensive health assessments for older people to detect and prevent health problems, either in their surgery or at the older person's home. You can encourage your parents to request this from their doctor.

What is a geriatrician?

Geriatricians are doctors who have done additional training in aged care. They specialise in the medical and lifestyle aspects of ageing.

The useful thing about geriatricians is that they undertake very comprehensive assessments of older people by investigating all the different aspects of the older person's health, well-being and lifestyle. They develop an overall understanding of the medical, pharmacological and social aspects of an older person and suggest the best course of action for the different issues, advising local doctors and other health care professionals who are involved. They can be valuable in working out the sort of care that your parent may need now or in the future.

If your parent is admitted to a public or private hospital and has numerous conditions that may affect or delay their discharge, then the treating doctor may refer them to a geriatrician. In Australia, geriatricians tend to be linked to organisations that specialise in aged care or rehabilitation, and like other medical specialists usually require a referral from the person's main doctor.

What is a rheumatologist?

A rheumatologist is a medical specialist physician whose area of expertise is the diagnosis and treating of diseases of the joints, muscles and bones. Rheumatologists help people who suffer with osteoarthritis and rheumatoid arthritis as well as other musculo-skeletal conditions. In treating and managing your parents' illness, the rheuma-tologist will work closely with the patient's general practitioner, as well as other skilled professionals, such as a physiotherapist, occupational therapist, psychologist or social worker. Nurses, podiatrists and dietitians may also form part of the team involved in your parents' treatment. Treatment options include physical therapy, general supportive care, drug treatment and surgery. Rheumatologists are generally attached to major public hospitals and may also have their own private practices. To find a rheumatologist in your area, contact the Australian Rheumatology Association in your state.

What is community care?

'Community care' is the term given to care at home, rather than care in a hospital or a residential facility such as a nursing home or hostel. It is the range of help and support that an older person might need and use to help them continue living in their own home. Community care is an extension of the care that traditionally might have been provided by close-knit families, social groups and friends. Today it comes from a wide range of government and public organisations, community based non-profit groups, church and welfare groups, and privately run organisations and businesses.

Some older people will need very little help, but others may find that they need a great deal of professional help and support to stay living at home. The time to consider getting outside help for your older parents is when things appear to be getting too much for them and for other family and friends to cope with. The best approach is to find out about services well in advance and not wait till the older person actually needs them. That way, when they are needed, you are well-informed, and, having already worked out the complexities of the aged-care system, can make satisfactory arrangements more easily.

Many community care services do not have enough resources or funding to allow them to provide services to everyone who would like them. This means that they need a way of assessing different people's circumstances to determine who should have priority and to whom they should provide the services. These decisions are influenced by government policies and rules and conditions attached to the funding from the government.

This means that most services have 'eligibility criteria' that are applied to help decide fairly who should get services. For example, eligibility criteria may include factors such as age, residential arrangements or income. They will vary between different services. As well as working out whether your elderly parent is eligible, there will be an assessment process to decide precisely what services the older person would benefit from, how often and when the situation should be reviewed.

The cost of community care will vary. It depends on what sort of help it is and to what extent it is government subsidised. As a general rule, most information, advice and assessments are free, but there are small charges for the actual services, often based on the older person's capacity to pay. Of course, if you use private services you will be charged commercial rates.

If your parent is assessed as ineligible for a service or considered a low priority and therefore unlikely to be provided with the service requested, you can ask the person who made that decision to describe the basis on which the decision was made. If you are not satisfied that the decision was fair to your parent, or if you think that the person making the decision was not aware of the full situation of your parent, you should ask that your parent be assessed again. If you still feel the decision is incorrect, you can ask the assessor how to go about making an appeal against the decision. Any service subsidised by government should have a documented complaints and appeals process and the service is required to inform you of that process, if requested.

The different sorts of community care services are described in detail in Chapter 6.

What does a home carer do?

A home carer is a health worker who comes into the home to assist the older person with health related or domestic tasks. Many home carers are subsidised by the government specifically to assist frail older people who are having difficulty managing at home. Home carers usually provide a set number of hours of assistance to the older person each week, depending on the type of assistance required. For example, they may provide one hour of house cleaning each week.

Home carers can help older people with personal grooming tasks such as bathing, showering and dressing, as well as everyday tasks around the home, such as house cleaning, laundry, shopping, meals, gardening or respite care so the carer can have a break.

For both public and private home care, the older person will undergo an assessment to determine the type and level of help they require.

Government subsidised home carers can be accessed through the Home and Community Care (HACC) program run in each state. This program is delivered through community-based organisations and councils across Australia. In addition to government subsidised home carers, home care can be privately purchased from some of the same organisations, as well as from other private organisations listed in the telephone book.

What does a support worker do?

A support worker is the general name given to a health or community worker who provides support to the older person. This term is often used in a general sense to include a home carer, respite worker or other health professional or worker who is providing some form of ongoing assistance to the older person. It can also mean a worker who has a role in providing information and advocacy in housing, legal or financial areas, or in dealing with authorities should you or your parents have a complaint to lodge.

What does an occupational therapist do for older people?

An occupational therapist is an allied health professional who works to maximise a person's functioning in and around their environment and increase their independence in personal, domestic, occupational and community activities. Occupational therapists assess the older person's physical and cognitive function and environment and develop treatment programs. Occupational therapists can assist older people to regain skills and functioning after illnesses or surgery, and can also make recommendations about the home environment and the use of any aids or equipment to help overcome difficulties that the person may be experiencing in doing tasks.

Occupational therapists can help older people:

- to identify and maintain the older person's ability for independent living
- to cope with age-related changes such as in vision, balance, coordination or energy
- by suggesting equipment and aids to assist the person in their daily life and to improve independence
- by making the home a safer place
- by assisting a person to manage while recovering from an illness such as stroke, arthritis or dementia
- by carrying out home assessments before a client's return home from hospital
- by developing ways to cope with memory loss
- by recommending or suggesting activities that will maintain the person's functioning
- to identify and use community resources and support services.

Occupational therapists are available in both the public and private systems. In the public system they are available through general hospitals (for older people who have been treated as a patient), rehabilitation hospitals, community health centres, day centres and Aged Care Assessment Teams.

Occupation Therapy Australia, the professional association for occupational therapists, can provide a list of occupational therapists in your area and those that specialise in working with older people. Check the telephone book for your state branch of Occupation Therapy Australia.

What does a physiotherapist do for older people?

A physiotherapist is involved in assessment, diagnosis and treatment related to physical movement. Older people often see a physiotherapist if they have been in hospital (for example, for a hip replacement), to ensure they regain maximum movement and mobility. Physiotherapists focus on problems associated with human movement and will recommend exercises to speed up recovery or re-habilitation and also work closely with occupational therapists where special equipment or gadgets are needed. They will assess, diagnose and plan a course of treatment for the older person.

Physiotherapists can help older people:

- with hands-on massage, manipulation and treatment
- with individual exercise and strength-building programs to help keep the older person fit and well and avoid age-related illnesses
- with gentle exercises to retain fitness and mobility, both at home or in groups, including strengthening, stretching, hydrotherapy, breathing, relaxation, and massage
- to reduce the pain and disability of conditions such as arthritis, osteoporosis, stroke, Parkinson's disease,

lymphoedema, asthma and chest troubles
- in recovery from falls, accidents and surgery
- by recommending safe movements such as the best way to get in and out of bed, bend over, sit and stand
- by recommending and/or providing equipment such as walking frames, wheelchairs, shower chairs and over-the-toilet chairs/frames to meet the older person's requirements and showing the older person how to use them safely.

Physiotherapists can be found in both the public and private systems. In the public system, they are available through general hospitals (for older people who have been treated as a patient), rehabilitation hospitals, community health centres and Aged Care Assessment Teams.

The Australian Physiotherapy Association can provide a list of physiotherapists in your area and those who specialise in working with older people. Check the telephone book for the number in your state.

What does a speech pathologist (therapist) do for older people?

Speech pathologists assess and treat people with speech and swallowing difficulties. This includes assisting people with all aspects of communication, including rehabilitation, or providing special communication equipment such as electronic aids. Assessments can include tolerance for liquids and solids, swallowing, hearing, reading and writing ability, ability to understand, verbal expression and memory.

Speech therapists can help older people:

- after injury or surgery
- to recover from illnesses including stroke
- suffering from dementia
- coping with Parkinson's disease
- experiencing general health decline

- to regain or optimise speech or communication ability
- to speak clearly, understand others and express their wishes
- by recommending simplifications in the older person's environment to assist in communication.

In situations where a person has had surgery, treatment or difficulties with swallowing, a speech therapist will often work closely with an occupational therapist to:

- address an older person's loss of ability or desire to feed themselves
- advise on swallowing techniques
- advise on related exercises
- advise on dietary alternatives
- reduce the likelihood of nutritional decline.

Speech therapists are available in the public system, through hospitals, community rehabilitation centres, community health centres and outpatient clinics. They are also available in the private system. Speech Pathology Australia, the professional association for speech pathologists, can advise you of speech therapists in your area who specialise in working with older people.

What does a dietitian do for older people?

Dietitians can help older people maintain a healthy, balanced and nutritional diet. This can be particularly important for older people who:

- are recovering from illness, accident or surgery and who require good nutrition to aid in the healing process
- require a specialised diet
- wish to lose weight, for example, to ease back or joint problems
- need to gain weight because of sudden weight loss and frailty
- live alone and are unused to preparing their own meals or disinclined to do so, for example, following the death of a partner.

Dietitians can be found at hospitals and community health centres. For private practitioners in your area, contact the Dietitians Association of Australia in your state.

What does a podiatrist do for older people?

A podiatrist is a health care professional who specialises in feet by diagnosing and treating ailments and conditions of the foot. For older people, feet are very important because of mobility and balance. The feet of older people can become neglected because they are difficult to reach and see, and old fingers can be too stiff or unskilled to manage scissors. So bending down to cut toenails can become an impossible task, and even dangerous if cuts lead to infections, or if faulty cutting leads to ingrown toenails.

The ability of a podiatrist to reduce or alleviate foot pain is crucial for motivating older people to move about. Podiatrists also make aids to prevent toes rubbing together, or against the shoe, and assess if particular footwear is needed. Community-based podiatrists work with older people to develop ways to assist them to care for their feet.

Podiatrists can help older people with:

- arthritis in the feet
- diabetes
- nail problems
- foot infections
- injuries below the knee
- the reduction of the pain of bunions by providing aids
- specialist or modified footwear, known as orthotics
- wounds or ulcers
- foot massage
- rehabilitation, as part of a rehabilitation team, or by providing foot-care after surgery
- advising about deteriorating foot conditions and options for treatment
- referring on for specialist treatment for serious foot ailments.

Podiatrists can be found at community health services, hospitals and medical clinics, and some local governments subsidise podiatry services at Senior Citizens Centres. Private podiatrists are listed in the telephone book. Some podiatrists, both private and publicly subsidised, make home visits if the older person is homebound.

There is an Australia-wide directory for access to publicly subsidised podiatry treatments. Check with the Australian Podiatry Association.

What does an audiologist do for older people?

An audiologist is a specialist in performing diagnostic audiological tests and managing the non-medical aspects of hearing problems. They provide hearing tests to determine what type of hearing loss the older person has and then offer advice and information about hearing aids and devices.

They can help older people who:

- have problems hearing in groups, or noisy or crowded situations
- have problems hearing when there is background noise
- need to turn up the television loudly to hear it
- ask people to repeat themselves, can't understand what other people are saying to them, or ask people to speak more loudly
- have trouble hearing the doorbell, telephone or alarms.

If your parents have hearing difficulties, you can assist by turning off or down any background noise, using soft furnishings to reduce echo, always facing the person you are speaking with, speaking slowly and clearly with short sentences and pauses, and giving the person time to respond.

Check the telephone book for the number for the Audiological Society of Australia or Better Hearing Australia in your state.

What does a psychologist do for older people?

A psychologist is a health professional who uses counselling and other techniques to help people with everyday problems such as major life changes, stress, relationship matters, and coping with illness.

Psychologists can help older people with:

- counselling for depression, bereavement and general coping skills
- assessments to determine cognitive (understanding, comprehension) and intellectual functioning
- behaviour modification
- sleeping difficulties
- eating and weight control problems.

The difference between a psychologist and a psychiatrist is that a psychiatrist has medical training, and can diagnose and prescribe medication for the treatment of mental illness in additional to any counselling techniques used.

Psychologists are available in the public system through some Aged Care Assessment Teams, rehabilitation services, hospitals, and community health services. They are also available in the private sector. The Australian Psychological Society Referral Service can refer you to a psychologist who specialises in working with older people in your area. Check the telephone book for the number in your state.

How can a social worker help older people?

A social worker assists people with the management of life's problems by focusing on the way people interact with others and society. They can discuss options and offer support and encouragement to people who want to deal with their life situation in a more satisfactory way. They can assist with problems relating to the family, finances, accommodation and personal and community relation-ships.

Social workers' area of expertise will vary depending on where they are employed. For example, a social worker in an acute care hospital will be involved in organising community services for a person going home after a period in hospital and assisting people to accept loss and change in their lives. In contrast, a social worker in a family support centre may specialise in family counselling, adolescent disputes or caring for older relatives. In a community health centre, a social worker may run preventative and health maintenance programs for individuals and groups as well as undertake personal counselling on a whole range of issues.

Nevertheless, regardless of where a social worker is located, they should have some knowledge about all other relevant services, pensions and benefits and, if they are not able to provide specific information in every area, they will be able to tell you who can. Welfare workers have slightly different qualifications but undertake very similar work; working with people trying to manage difficulties in their lives.

Social workers or welfare workers can assist older people and their families with:

- getting on with other family members and making important decisions
- counselling for depression, loss and grief
- ensuring that all benefits and concessions have been applied for
- advice about services in their area and providing contact names and numbers
- managing crises such as accident or illness in terms of the older person's overall situation and circumstances, such as going home from hospital
- advocating for the older person
- arranging support and care.

To find out about social workers in your area who work with older people, contact your local hospital or community health centre. Social workers also work in private practice and the Australian Association of Social Workers, listed in the telephone book, can provide a list of practitioners in your area.

What does a community nurse do?

A community nurse is a nurse who works with people and provides them with nursing care in their own home (rather than in a hospital or other medical facility). Community nurses are available to assist older people living in the community and can provide a range of health services, from highly specialised care such as the use of intravenous drips, feeding tubes, catheters and complex wound care, to assisting with personal care and management of hygiene.

Community nurses can also assist with:

- managing medication
- managing diabetes and other chronic conditions
- managing bladder problems (see continence advisers)
- assessing and managing memory problems
- cancer care and support
- stomal care (which involves care of the stomal site, hygiene, advice on the changing of the bags and information about nutrition).

Nurses will often work in collaboration with staff from home care services; for example the home care service provides the personal care while the nurses provide more complex care.

For most older people, their first contact with community nurses occurs following discharge from hospital, particularly today when people are being discharged from hospital earlier. Patients are referred by the hospital or by their local doctor, but can also refer themselves to most community nursing services, or a family member, a doctor or another health professional may do so. However, if the patient care involves taking medication or invasive procedures such as catheters, a medical authorisation will need to be obtained by the nursing service from the patient's doctor.

In metropolitan areas, community nurses are available in the public system through specific nursing services such as Royal District Nursing Service (Victoria and South Australia) and Blue Nursing (Queensland) and through local community health centres. In regional or rural areas, community nurses often work from the local hospital or, again, the community health centre. There are also a number of private nursing services, for which rebates may be available under private health insurance.

Public community nursing services are subsidised by government. Fees range from $2.50 per hour for pensioners. Most nursing services will 'cap' the amount pensioners need to pay in any one month to around $30. For non-pensioners, fees are often charged on a sliding scale depending on the patient's income level. For some non-pensioners with private health insurance, private nursing services may be a recommended option.

What is a continence adviser?

Continence advisers are nurses who have been specially trained to provide assistance to people concerned about incontinence. Many older people generally, as well as those with dementia, and men with prostate problems, experience incontinence. Incontinence can vary from waking twice or more during the night to go to the toilet, to leakage of small amounts of urine when coughing, laughing or being active, through to more serious involuntary loss of control of the bladder or bowel. These problems can often be cured or significantly improved. Continence nurse advisers provide information and advice about treatment and aids.

What is an assessment officer?

Most services require older people to be assessed before they provide services to them. Assessments are used to collect information about the older person and their needs

so that the health worker can make diagnoses and identify the treatment, assistance or care that the person requires. Following assessment, a care plan for the older person is usually devised in conjunction with the older person and other relevant family members. To do an assessment, the worker will usually visit the older person at home to ask questions and look at the living environment, speak to other family members and involve other health professionals or specialists, including the older person's doctor, as may be required.

Assessments will vary from one service to another and from one health professional to another. They may include consideration of and collecting information about:

- contact details such as the name, date of birth, address, phone number and religion of the older person, and contact details for the carer or person who made the initial inquiry
- the physical capabilities of the older person
- the older person's medical history
- the cognitive (understanding, comprehension, perception) ability of the older person
- the emotional and mental health status of the older person
- their living environment
- their ability to undertake everyday tasks and to look after themselves

- support services that might have been used in the past or that the older person is currently using
- support that is, or can be, provided by family and friends
- income levels
- the wishes and preferences of the older person and their willingness to accept help.

If your older parents need assistance from a number of different services, you may find that they are required to have a number of different assessments. The older person can request that the information collected by one assessment worker or service be shared with other assessment workers or services, so that the process is not repeated unnecessarily.

What is a case manager?

At some stage, the older person may be receiving a number of different services from different health professionals and agencies. A 'case manager' is the title given to the worker whose role it is to coordinate all the different health workers and services involved in the older person's care, and to liaise with the older person and their family to ensure that the situation is progressing according to everyone's wishes. The case manager will develop a 'care plan' (a plan that lists the support services the older person needs) that outlines all the different services and who is responsible for which aspects of the care plan. In some cases, the case manager also has a pool of funds which can be used to purchase extra community support services (such as home nursing, respite care, meals and so on) if these are needed for the person.

The case manager will monitor the arrangements put in place for the older person over time, and assist with issues as they arise. They will negotiate with the different health workers and support services to increase or decrease the amount of service being provided or to suggest and bring in new services as they are required.

Case managers are usually trained social workers, nurses (or similar) and, as such, work very closely with the older person and their family to ensure everyone involved is satisfied with the arrangements.

If your older parent is involved with and receiving services from a number of different agencies, or has very complex needs and requires a person to coordinate their care, and you think they would benefit from a case manager, you may find out what case managers are available in your area. Public services that do provide case managers have quite strict eligibility requirements and probably have waiting lists, so you will need to demonstrate your older parent's frailty and the complex needs arising from their situation.

When you make enquiries and request a case manager, you should be aware that:

- you will need to provide a fair amount of detail over the telephone and be able to describe the older person's circumstances and their needs
- the case manager will need to come and visit the older person, preferably with you present, and make an assessment of the situation
- there may be a waiting list (and you should phone and check where your parent's name is on it)
- there may be fees or charges.

Not all support services have case managers, however they are available through some parts of both the public health system and the private sector. Case managers in the public system are funded by the government and may be attached to a variety of programs which cater for clients with complex needs, or for recipients of aged-care packages, as explained in Chapter 10. Usually, there is no income test applied so anyone can access them.

You can act as the case manager for your older parents if you wish to do so. This will mean that you take responsibility for all the organising, coordinating and monitoring of their care (including making referrals to services, organising for health workers to do assessments, coordinating the plan of care). Also you will need to remain in close communication and discussion with the different services and health workers involved. Depending on the complexity of the situation, this may require a large amount of time and commitment from you. Many family members do choose to act as the case manager or coordinator for their older parent.

Some private agencies also provide case managers. Look in the telephone book under 'Nursing' and ask the businesses listed there if they provide case managers. As privately owned enterprises, they will charge a fee for providing a case manager and for the work the case manager undertakes.

How can the pharmacist help?

Off with the white coat and out from behind the counter! Many pharmacists are changing the way they have traditionally practised. As well as dispensing medicines, they are increasingly providing other information and support for customers. For older people, this is especially valuable, as good pharmacists should now:

- be prepared to sit down with older people and discuss their different medications
- answer any questions about the medication and how the different drugs might interact with each other
- point out any possible side effects
- suggest 'generic' brands of medicines: exactly the same drug but in an unbranded package so that it is often considerably cheaper
- speak with the older person's doctor if they, or you, have any concerns about the medication
- provide information about support services that may be available in your area.

Pharmacists can receive payment from the government to undertake 'medication reviews' for older people who are taking a number of medications regularly. This involves visiting the older person, looking at their medicines, and making sure they are all up to date, work together well, and that any side effects will be manageable. This is especially useful for older people who have been taking a number of medicines. If your older parent or relative takes several drugs regularly and has a cupboard at home with lots of medication (some of which might be quite old!) why not think about a medication review and dispose of all out-of-date medications? To arrange one, simply ask the pharmacists whether they do in-home, or domiciliary, medication reviews. A referral by a doctor is required.

The pharmacy profession also has a phone-in day once a year when members of the general public can phone in and ask questions about their medication.

So, think of the pharmacist as another helper in the support and care of the older person.

What is an Aged Care Assessment Service or Team?

An Aged Care Assessment Service (or Team) is the name given to a Commonwealth Government program that is responsible for assessing older people prior to:

- entry into nursing homes (known as high-level care)
- entry into hostels (known as low-level care)
- the provision of a community aged-care or extended aged-care package that can provide up to the same level of care and support that the older person would get if they were living in a hostel or nursing home, but it is provided in the person's own home instead
- provision of some respite care.

Because nursing homes and hostels are very expensive for the government, with each 'bed' or person living in a nursing home costing up to $50,000 per year (most of which is paid for by taxpayers), the government is quite strict about who can enter.

Aged Care Assessment Teams have the responsibility to approve applications for the services listed above. When being spoken about, Aged Care Assessment Teams or Services are often shortened to ACAT or ACAS.

ACAS (ACAT) employ teams of skilled health prof-essionals. These teams usually include a mix of different health professionals including a geriatrician, an occup-ational therapist, a social worker, nurses and physio-therapists. They will undertake a very detailed and comprehensive assessment of the older person and their situation.

The purpose of the assessment undertaken by the assessment worker is to work out the care that the older person needs, and identify and link them with the services that can respond and assist with those needs. Based on the assessment, the ACAS (ACAT) will:

- help an older person and their family decide if the older person cannot manage in their own home and needs assistance
- recommend what level of care the older person needs
- assess whether the older person requires the level of care provided by a nursing home, hostel or a package
- make recommendations about moving into residential care, if necessary, and provide advice and information about residential care services, such as nursing homes and hostels in the preferred area
- assess whether the older person is eligible to access these services and how urgent their needs are
- suggest appropriate residential facilities (nursing home or hostel) or community care services for you to contact
- provide information and advice about respite care.

Visits, assessments and advice by Aged Care Assessment workers are fully subsidised by the government and are free. You do not have to agree with their assessment or act on their recommendations. ACAS (ACAT) are often located at or near public hospitals, particularly those that focus on aged-care or rehabilitation. To find your nearest

ACAS (ACAT), check the key contact list towards the end of Chapter 6.

What is a recreation or activities officer?

These are people located in local government, church groups and clubs, to ensure that appropriate leisure activities exist for the range of ages and types of people in the local community. If your area does have such a person, the activities they develop range across walking, exercise and dance groups, gardening and learning opportunities (such as how to operate a computer), singing and special interest groups of all types, a wide variety of indoor and outdoor games and sports. Senior citizens clubs, libraries and public halls are likely venues for these activities. In addition, a recreation or activities officer may assist individuals who are attempting to rejoin activities after some traumatic event like an illness or injury, and they may be located at a community health or rehabilitation centre.

What does the Guardianship and Administration Board do for older people?

The Guardianship and Administration Board is a statutory body with the power to make important decisions on behalf of people who are unable to do so themselves. There must be strong evidence that the person in question is unable to make these decisions themselves. The Board has the power to appoint a guardian (to make lifestyle decisions) and/or an administrator (to make financial decisions and manage the person's financial affairs) who is then given the power to make decisions on behalf of that person. The Board can appoint another family member, a friend, or the Public Trustee as guardian or administrator. For older people, these important decisions are likely to be in relation to living circumstances, finances and property. Some states also have an Office of the Public Advocate which has a complementary role.

Check the telephone book for the Guardianship and/or Administration Board and/or Office of the Public Advocate in your state.

Other health professionals

There are, of course, other health professionals who may be involved in working with older people. Your parents may have a number treating them at the same time. In this situation, be sure to ask each health professional to explain their role and how they coordinate and communicate with other health professionals. It is also wise to ask if any one health professional has been designated as having the lead role and if this is the person you or your parents should contact if they are concerned about any aspect of their treatment, or any adverse reaction to it.

No service in your area?

If the service your parents need is not available in your area, why not contact your state government, local politicians and community groups about developing the service in future.

6 Help is on the way

About services — what's available to help older people (and you) and how to get your fair share

Poem

Now I'm nearly fifty,
my mother's seventy-three
I have recently been pondering,
should she live with me?
I love my mother dearly,
that no-one can deny
but at the thought of living together again
I cannot help but sigh.
She's a little bit forgetful,
quite doddery and grey
but will absolutely insist
on me doing things her way.
We have some common interests,
gardening we both enjoy
she would plant some violets
and I would plant bok choy.
Beef vindaloo, hot chilli,
bean curd and sushi I prefer,
but chops and three boiled vegies
is the menu to suit her.
So here is a dilemma —
how can she live alone?
Perhaps I can get services
to support her in her home!

Author unknown

Most older people live independently in their own homes. However, as they continue to get older, they may find they need some extra help.

Many older people start to worry when they have difficulty keeping up with tasks around the house or being able to move freely around the house. They see it as a sign of their ageing and inability to cope. They may not ask for help but struggle on until other family members notice and offer assistance.

Quite often difficulty in managing daily life can be because of physical reasons related to getting older, for example because of arthritis, a sore hip, a sore back, or poor eyesight. This means that older people may have difficulty bending over to do tasks, experience pain, or simply tire easily and not have the energy required.

For many frail older people, medical and physical conditions underlie or contribute to them depending on others to complete many of the daily and household tasks we take for granted.

Is help needed?

There are many services to help older people stay living comfortably at home. If you are considering using support services for your older parents, some questions you should discuss with them first are:

- What can they comfortably do by themselves?
- What do they most want help with?
- Are other family members available to provide some of this help on a regular (weekly or fortnightly) basis?
- What are absolutely the most important things to get help with?
- What will make the biggest contribution to their sense of well-being, comfort and safety?

You may wish to use the checklist on the following page to discuss these questions with your older parents and to highlight where help might be needed.

Daily living skill	Manages well	Just gets by	Needs help now	Will need help in in future
Packing or retrieving food from lower shelf of the fridge				
Wheeling the supermarket trolley				
Getting the shopping home and unpacked				
Lifting heavy/full pots and pans from stove to bench top				
Unscrewing jars, peeling vegetables				
Preparing and cooking adequate meals				
Changing the bed				
Noticing when clothes and bed linen require washing				
Doing the washing				
Hanging wet washing on the line				
Getting dry washing off the line				
Ironing or deciding to use clothes unironed				
Sweeping or mopping floors				
Using the vacuum cleaner				
Cleaning the shower				
Cleaning the bath				
Cleaning the toilet				
Cleaning the stove and oven				
Using the telephone				
Banking in general				
Using an automatic teller machine				
Understanding and attending to mail received				
Putting out the rubbish and bringing in the empty bin				
Getting to shops, libraries, banks etc.				
Managing finances				
Taking medication according to instructions				
Picking up dropped articles from the floor				
Keeping track of day and date and keeping appointments				
Maintaining personal hygiene				

Discuss with your parents what their answers on this checklist could indicate about their ability to live alone, and where they may require help, either now or in the future.

If your older parents require assistance with several of the items above, it may be time to organise some help for them. Or it may be that the older person would benefit from moving into a smaller home that is more manageable and designed with low maintenance and older people in mind.

Practical help

There is a range of services available that provide practical help at home to assist older people with everyday domestic tasks, health-related tasks and generally to assist older people to remain living comfortably in their own home for as long as they choose to do so. There are many services available through the public system and heavily subsidised by the government so that the cost to the older person is minimal. Many services are also available through the private sector and private practitioners, who will charge market rates. In some instances, rebates may be available through private health funds. This chapter focuses on public services that are available and subsidised by the government, especially to assist older people remain living safely in their own homes. However, although a vast range of services to help older people do exist, it may not mean that you can get all the help you want or need for your older parent.

How to get your fair share

Services available will vary somewhat from one area to another across Australia. When you have read this chapter, you will be amazed at the number and type of services available. However, it is not as easy as it might sound; services often have quite long waiting lists, require people to be assessed as eligible to use the service, and because they are so busy, may prove difficult to contact. You should also note that services may not be as well coordinated or as efficient as you might expect.

If you wish to use subsidised services, you will need to:

- spend time finding out about and understanding the different sorts of services available in your parents' area
- be assertive and friendly, not aggressive or frustrated when you are trying to find out information
- be prepared to answer questions and describe the sort of help that the older person needs and what they can and cannot do
- be proactive and ask about services rather than waiting for the health worker to suggest them
- ask questions such as 'What else might be available to help people in our situation?' or 'What other support services are available in this area?'
- be prepared to spend time talking with health workers on many different occasions
- be prepared for multiple assessments that may require a lot of your time, in supporting your older parents through the processes
- be persistent and don't give up too easily
- start a folder or file in which to collate all your notes and information.

Hurdles

Care at home can be arranged for older people, right through from those who need just a small amount of help to those who need a great deal of support, and who might otherwise be placed in a nursing home or hostel. However, you should be aware that there may be waiting lists for most services, so the sooner you find out about them the better informed you will be about when services might be available to help your older parents.

Because many of the services are unable to help everybody who might need help, they may try to 'put you off' by using the following tactics to help them ration their service:

- being too busy to call you back
- insisting on another assessment
- asking for a referral from a doctor when you are able to make the referral yourself
- suggesting that you may not be eligible
- telling you of their long waiting lists.

However, all services are there to help those that are most in need, so if your elderly parents require help, be aware of these tactics and calmly proceed to follow through with your inquiries and request the relevant assessment or action.

If your parent lives in an isolated or rural area or if for any other reason you simply cannot track down the service you want in your area, then contact the office of your local state and/or federal Member of Parliament. Staff in these offices have access to a wealth of information and an interest in helping you solve your problem.

Assessment

Most aged-care services use an assessment process to help them decide:

- whether or not the older person needs their support services
- precisely what sort of services they need
- how much they require
- the relative urgency of one applicant's needs against other applicants' needs
- whether the service has the capacity to provide what the older person needs
- whether other services or health professionals should be involved.

The assessment process is likely to involve at a minimum:
- asking for detailed information over the telephone about the older person (for example, when you make an enquiry)
- a discussion with the older person and relevant others (such as partner, relatives, doctor or other health professional as appropriate) about what assistance they require
- a visit by the service to meet the older person and assess their ability to undertake tasks (refer to Aged Care Assessment Service in the previous chapter).

The health worker undertaking the assessment will consider all the information gained through the process and make a recommendation and decision about whether or not to offer services. The information will be recorded by the worker in a confidential file retained by the service, and with the older person's permission can be shared with other services or health workers whom you may be approaching for assistance. A copy of the assessment and file information can be requested by the older person themselves.

Deciding what you want

When you contact an organisation about assistance for your older parents, you want to be sure that it will provide high-quality service. You should follow these simple steps:

Step 1 Contact the organisation and describe the older person's needs and the sort of help you are looking for. Ask about the different services they offer and get them to send you any information they have.

Step 2 Discuss the information they provide with your older parents and think about what you all want, then decide what would be most helpful.

Step 3 Contact the organisation again and ask for any additional information you need; you may have more specific questions (see Chapter 7). Arrange a visit to the service to look around or ask them to come and visit you and your older parent.

Step 4 Make a decision and apply to receive the service, following whatever application and assessment process the service may have.

Step 5 Monitor the arrangements and make sure both your older parents and you are happy with them and that they are likely to meet your parents' needs as they change over time.

Step 6 Go back to the supervisor or initial assessor if you find that the plan for your parents is fine but it fails in the implementation for reasons such as the worker not being allowed to do their task or your parents not getting along with the worker.

You may find that help from more than one organisation is best to provide everything that you need.

What the government funds or subsidises

The Commonwealth Government contributes more than $3 billion per year to aged care, and state governments, local councils and other organisations add significantly to this. The Home and Community Care program, known as HACC, is a major government program to assist older people and their carers (and younger people with disabilities) across Australia to stay living at home. Generally, people aged over 65 years are eligible to receive

HACC services, provided they are assessed as needing assistance. Usually there is no income or assets test, so the service is equally available to all older people in need. However, fees are on a sliding scale which, at the top end, may almost be equal to private enterprise charges. HACC services cannot always keep up with demand so there are often waiting lists and priority is given to those with the most urgent needs.

The government also funds residential care, such as nursing homes and hostels, and the community-based equivalents of these. That is, the same level of care (or equivalent funding) is provided for a person should they be living in a nursing home or hostel, or in their own home in the community. This information is covered in Chapter 10.

Other government assistance for older people includes programs for carers, programs for veterans, financial assistance and community support services.

The types of services and organisations available to help older people are listed below. Details about what the service provides and where to find out more about it are given on the following pages.

You should note that the names and availability of services will vary somewhat across Australia. You should also note that, while many of these services are heavily subsidised by government, the cost will vary from area to area.

List of services

Information is provided about the following services:

- home care, home help and housekeeping
- property and home and garden maintenance and/or modification
- food and meal-on-wheels or delivered meals
- Senior Citizens Centres
- home health care, paramedical or allied health, community nursing, personal care

- day care, day activity services and social support
- respite care
- friendly visiting
- case management for people who need a lot of care or assistance
- transport
- rehabilitation
- vision and hearing
- falls prevention
- information services
- support for carers
- personal alarms
- help for people with dementia
- help for people with arthritis
- help for veterans (returned soldiers and their partners)
- financial help
- palliative care for the terminally ill
- other useful organisations
- help for the middle-aged person worrying about their older parents.

Home care, home help and housekeeping

Home care or home help is a government program that provides help with regular house cleaning and household jobs. It is available for frail older people through the HACC program. The government's aim is to keep frail older people living independently in their own home and in a safe and comfortable environment for as long as possible.

The type of assistance provided will depend on the needs of the older person and what they can and cannot do themselves, their preferences, the results of their assessment, and what the service is able to offer. What is available differs between states and services, but typically includes regular cleaning tasks such as:

- vacuuming
- cleaning bathrooms and toilets
- mopping floors
- dusting
- washing and ironing
- changing bed linen
- cleaning stoves and fridges.

As well, help with tasks such as shopping, banking or meal preparation may be available.

Many older people use home care services for many years, and get to know the worker or workers involved. They look forward to their weekly or fortnightly visit and welcome the contact with the worker.

The advantages of using HACC home care include the following: staff must have a minimum level of training (gained through TAFE College) to work with older people; the service is heavily subsidised by the government, with a small hourly fee charged; and the staff will help in monitoring the overall well-being of the older person. However, there are also disadvantages.

In comparison to a privately employed house cleaner, HACC home care workers have much stricter guidelines (for occupational health and safety reasons) about what they can and cannot do. For example, they may not be able to assist with changing light bulbs, cleaning windows or blinds, or moving furniture to vacuum underneath it, or they may be allowed only to vacuum not sweep. Also, restrictions are likely on the amount of home care that is provided — usually an hour or less each week or fortnight — and because of demand, there may be a waiting period.

As a HACC service, home care is heavily subsidised by

the government, with a small fee payable. A HACC service costs significantly less than purchasing these services privately. For information on HACC contact details, refer to the table of key contact numbers towards the end of this chapter.

Property and home and garden maintenance and/or modification

Property or home maintenance is a program similar to home care, but it focuses on the heavier duty tasks around the home and garden. It is available for frail older people through the HACC program. The government's aim of assisting frail older people with household and property maintenance is, once again, to keep them living independently in their own home and in a safe environment for as long as possible.

Older people often begin to feel that they are not coping when they are no longer able to keep up with the lawns or gardening. This relatively simple service can make a big difference to the older person. Alternatively, they may wish to move into a smaller property that has fewer maintenance requirements and less garden to look after!

The type of assistance provided will depend on the needs of the older person and what they can and cannot do themselves, the type of property, the results of their assessment, and what the service is able to offer. Typically, property or home maintenance assistance can include:

- lawn mowing
- gardening tasks such as pruning, raking, weeding
- cleaning gutters
- spring cleaning
- installing rails
- installing smoke alarms and replacing batteries
- chopping firewood
- replacing tap and toilet washers
- changing light globes

- clearing spouting
- cutting back shrubs from pathways
- unblocking drains
- advising in respect of any major repairs required
- minor carpentry.

Apart from lawn mowing, these tasks tend to be done on a less regular or once-only basis. Like other HACC services, they are heavily subsidised by the government, with a small fee charged.

There are also services that assist with larger home maintenance tasks, such as painting, repairs, fixing cracks in driveways or footpaths, installing security screens or altering bathrooms for safety reasons.

In Victoria, there is the Home Inspection and Home Renovation Scheme for Older People. The home inspection service can check older people's homes for maintenance needs and to ensure a safe home environment. The home renovation service helps older people remain independent in their own home.

The service will suggest home improvements and modifications to assist the older person to continue living in safety. Independent advisers provide a free inspection and written condition report with cost estimates. It is then up to the older person and their family as to whether they proceed to have the works carried out.

Renovations could, for example, include:

- ramps for easy access
- grab rails in the bathroom
- safety showers without steps
- grab rails near the front and/or back verandah stairs
- safe non-slip floor coverings
- better lighting and security lighting
- fencing and gates
- roof tiling
- electrical work
- plumbing
- heater replacement.

In some states, the government provides low-cost loans to assist people on low incomes to carry out home maintenance, repair or modifications. For contact details, refer to the table of key contact numbers towards the end of this chapter.

Food, meals-on-wheels or delivered meals

Sometimes older people find it difficult to cook for themselves. There are various ways that food or assistance can be provided. Many people have heard of meals-on-wheels, meals that are delivered to elderly people who are, for a range of reasons, unable to cater for themselves, or do not wish to do so, either for a short period or over the longer term.

For example:

- Older people coming home from hospital may be unable to cook meals.
- Older people may have a physical condition or disability which restricts them from shopping and cooking.
- The older person may have an illness.
- The older person may simply be too frail to cope with the tasks of buying food and preparing meals.
- The older person may never have learned to cook.

Delivered meals through the HACC program usually consist of up to three courses: an entrée (such as soup); a main course (such as a roast dinner or fish and vegetables); and a dessert (such as yoghurt and fruit). Often fruit juice is also provided. The meals are delivered in advance, either already heated (if the person is going to consume them straight away) or chilled ready to be heated. They are usually packaged in foil trays, and can be transferred onto a dinner plate for heating in the microwave or oven.

The advantages of delivered meals are that they are nutritionally balanced, can cater for special dietary requirements and cultural preferences, are subsidised and inexpensive, are available seven days per week (delivered in advance), and may be ordered as often or as infrequently as you wish. The disadvantages are that they are not cooked in the older person's kitchen by family members, they do not require the older person's participation in their preparation and, like all mass-produced food, they may be different in taste and texture from what the older person is used to.

As well as meals delivered to the older person's home, there are other options to assist with good eating habits:

- Help with shopping and food preparation or cooking at home can be provided by some home care services.
- Group and social meals are often available at local venues and day centres that run lunch clubs specifically for older people who wish to enjoy a meal in a social setting.

Meals-on-wheels are subsidised through the HACC program. Their cost will vary around Australia but is likely to be in the vicinity of $5 to $7 per three-course meal. For information about HACC-delivered meals, contact the HACC number, for your state, listed toward the end of this chapter.

Many private enterprise organisations produce meals that can be purchased and delivered to older people, at rates that are often surprisingly reasonable, especially if purchased in packs of ten or so that can be kept frozen until needed.

There are also a great variety of pre-cooked meals available from supermarkets, including fat-reduced options. Compared with buying and cooking for one person, these pre-cooked alternatives can be economical and provide a good variety.

Senior Citizens Centres

Most people have heard of Senior Citizens Centres or Clubs which are well established across Australia. They provide a meeting place for senior citizens groups and encourage people to meet socially. They are often a mine of information about 'the system' and all the concessions that older people may be entitled to and how to get the best from a variety of services such as public transport and Centrelink.

Senior Citizens Clubs offer a variety of activities which may include:

- meals
- government-subsidised services eg. podiatry, transport
- games and activities
- outings
- indoor bowls
- singing
- classes eg. sewing, art, embroidery, gardening.

Many of these groups represent different nationalities and often offer meals that are specifically prepared according to different ethnic tastes, sometimes by the participants themselves. The provision of subsidised meals has become more flexible over the years in response to the opportunity to create an enjoyable social occasion as well as ensure an adequate meal. Check with your local council or library about Senior Citizens Clubs available in your area.

Home health care, nursing and personal care

The HACC program also provides personal carers that offer assistance with daily personal care tasks. HACC further provides allied health services (such as nursing, physiotherapy, occupational therapy, podiatry, speech therapy, counselling) to older people to assist them to remain living independently at home.

Frail older people may have difficulty in undertaking daily personal care and grooming tasks, due to rehabilitation, chronic illness, immobility or disability. A personal care worker or community nurse can help an older person who may require assistance:

- with bathing, showering or toileting
- with dressing and undressing
- with sitting up, turning around, and getting in and out of a bed, chair or vehicle
- with eating and drinking
- with shaving and grooming.

Because of scarce resources, it may be that a request for personal care assistance is refused on the grounds that a physically able person is living in the household and could perform the required task. In this situation, if it is inappropriate for a variety of reasons for this person to undertake the personal care tasks, you and your parents should ensure that the assessor, or person making the decision about providing the service, understands these reasons so that the request for service is reconsidered.

Allied health workers and nurses visit and work with the older person in their own home, or at a community health centre, rehabilitation centre or other health venue.

For example:

- Home visiting nurses will assist older people who have been discharged from hospital, have an illness or a wound that needs dressing, or who require injections or medication.
- Dietitians can assist older people who live alone, are not eating well, and/or require help to prepare food of a specific texture and nutritional value following an illness or surgery.
- An occupational therapist can assess the older person's home environment and suggest aids and equipment to make sure the person can function to the best of their ability in the home and ensure it is as safe as possible. Recommendations may include rails in the bathroom or ramps instead of steps.
- A physiotherapist may provide some hands-on therapy in the home and may recommend and arrange for hydrotherapy for an older person with arthritis or other physical disabilities.

- Information can be provided on the management of health problems such as diabetes or incontinence.
- Bereavement counselling can be offered to an older person whose partner has died.

Like other HACC services, these services will only be available after an assessment. As services are subsidised by the government, only a small fee is charged.

Similar services can be purchased privately from private health practitioners. Contact the HACC number for your state, listed towards the end of this chapter, for information about these services.

Day care, day activity services and social support

For older people who live alone, maintaining some social networks is an important consideration. Day care takes people out of their home for the day to participate in organised group and social activities. Because day centre programs usually run for four to five hours, they almost provide a 'day off' for the usual carer, giving the much-needed opportunity for both parties to spend time with people outside the family, people with whom they share some common interests or who are at least in the same age group. Most centres are open during the middle of the day and also provide a meal. Some have their own transport and can collect people from their homes and take them back at the end of the session. Some day centres also offer assistance with personal care activities such as toileting.

Day care centres run social support and activity programs that encourage the older person to participate in interesting group activities with their peers. The aim is to enhance their physical, social and emotional well-being. Centres vary in size but all offer a wide range of activity and social groups. Activities can include centre-based games, cards, bingo, crafts, quizzes and exercises, as well as outings and entertainments.

Group activities are organised by a group coordinator, who runs a range of interesting programs designed for:

- older people generally, who are still relatively independent but wish to participate in group activities
- frail older people who have dementia and require stimulation and supervision.

Day care centres can be run by local councils, voluntary, church-based or community organisations. There is usually a small charge for attending a day centre which you should ask about when you contact them. For further information, start by contacting the HACC number for your state, listed towards the end of this chapter.

Respite care

'Respite care' is the term given to the provision of short-term and temporary care (ranging from one hour to several weeks) that allows both:

- the people who normally look after or care for the older person to have a break
- and the older person themselves to have a break from their normal routine.

Respite care is flexible and can be provided in various ways, for example:

- a worker comes to look after the older person in their home while the carer has a break or goes out
- the older person leaves home and attends and participates in a day activity group for several hours during the middle of the day
- the respite care worker takes the older person out
- the respite care worker stays overnight in the older person's home to care for them
- the older person goes to stay in a residential facility (such as a nursing home, special accommodation service or hostel) for a short period.

Respite care can be organised either on a regular basis, such as once a week or once a month, or in emergency situations or when unplanned events occur that mean the usual carer is not available.

Residential respite care involves the carer being given a break while the older person stays in a nursing home or hostel. This type of respite is limited to 63 days per year in a Commonwealth-funded residential facility and the person must be assessed by an Aged Care Assessment Team. People under the Department of Veterans Affairs are eligible for an additional 28 days residential respite care in a private facility, and on discharge from hospital to an additional 21 days in a private facility for convalescence.

Fees for respite care will vary according to the type of respite care being used.

Friendly visiting

Friendly visiting services are non-profit organisations (usually assisted by some government funding) that train volunteers to act as friendly visitors for people who would otherwise be isolated in their homes. There is usually a coordinator who will discuss the reasons for the request with the older person or a relative making the enquiry. The coordinator will want to know:

- the reason the person wants a visitor
- the age and gender of the person
- their interests and any special attributes
- any special requests or preferences about the visitor, for example, they prefer a man, a woman, a young person, an older person, someone who will read to them.

The coordinator usually then visits the older person to further discuss their preferences, suitable day and time, frequency, and possibly an activity to be undertaken. Activities could include a board game, a walk around the garden, discussion on news items, sports and the like, or just a friendly conversation. There is usually no charge for the service and the visitor is often the high point of an older person's week. Check with your local HACC or Red Cross services about the friendly visiting service in your area.

Community options

For some older people, the provision of some delivered meals, home nursing or house cleaning is not enough; they have more complicated needs. In these cases, there are services specially designed to provide higher levels of care and a larger amount and number of services than those listed above. These special services — known as 'Community Options' (and sometimes 'Linkages' in Victoria) — are case management and/or brokerage services.

Basically these services work with older people to coordinate and broker or purchase the whole range of services needed to support them living at home because of complex care needs.

Qualified health professionals, known as case or care managers (see Chapter 5 for their role), undertake a comprehensive assessment of the older person's needs and develop a plan of care to support them. This plan of care is worked out with the older person and their family and then closely monitored to ensure that the services are meeting the older person's needs. The care plan is then updated as these needs change, and services are increased, decreased or introduced as required.

The case manager allocates to the care of each older person a pool of funds from which they negotiate and purchase the services required. The funds allocated each year to the older person will vary according to their needs, but the average amount is $10,000.

Services organised, purchased and coordinated by the case manager for a frail older person or person with dementia can include:

- respite care
- home nursing
- supporting the carer
- household cleaning and tasks
- transport
- personal care.

As for other services, an older person's eligibility to receive these services will depend on an assessment. There may also be waiting lists as these services are very much in demand.

The service is heavily subsidised by the government and fees are charged on a sliding scale and based on the older person's capacity to pay. For information about these services, contact the HACC program in your state.

Story

*M*R AND MRS SMITH *live in a unit in an inner suburb, and are aged 84 years and 77 years respectively. Mrs Smith has Parkinson's disease and Mr Smith had been her primary carer. He had been assisting with her personal care, organising medication, and doing the shopping and cooking. They have a private arrangement for fortnightly home care. Mr Smith has recently suffered a stroke which has left him with some left-sided weakness and short-term memory problems.*

Mr and Mrs Smith have a private income which precludes them from receiving a pension, although their income is only marginally more than the cut-off point.

They have two supportive daughters. One daughter lives in country Victoria, the other lives 20 minutes drive from her parents and works three days per week. The daughters have joint enduring powers of attorney for both their parents.

The two daughters were very concerned about the ability of their parents to remain at home. Mr Smith was insisting he could continue caring for his wife and this was placing a strain on the daughters who had been sharing the care of their mother since their father was admitted to hospital at the time of the stroke. The hospital social worker had offered to organise services and to refer both parents to a Community Options program. Mr Smith had refused these arrangements.

One daughter contacted the Community Options program and advised that Mr Smith had agreed (although reluctantly and only after considerable persuasion from herself, her sister and their mother) to a visit from the case manager to discuss the services available. This daughter was informed that there was a waiting list, however the case manager took the referral details over the phone and explained the referral/intake process. The case manager also offered to refer the parents to the local government to commence services. The daughter stated that her father was not agreeable to this but that they could continue assisting their parents until the case manager visited.

Six weeks later, the family (Mr and Mrs Smith and the two daughters) were visited by the case manager. This resulted in them reluctantly accepting a Linkages package for Mrs Smith. The case manager proceeded to visit regularly, developed a rapport with the family, and services were slowly increased. After a few months, clients Mr and Mrs Smith were initiating direct contact with the case manager on a regular basis.

Transport: getting around

Parking permit

An older car driver with significant physical limitation can apply through their local government or shire offices for a disabled parking permit. The application must be supported by medical evidence detailing disability, and if the permit is granted the person will be supplied with a sticker entitling them to park in areas marked for disabled parking.

If the disabled person is not a driver, they can apply for a parking permit that covers someone else driving them. The sticker is distinctive and any parking officer coming across it would expect to see an able driver and a disabled passenger.

Public transport

This varies enormously across Australia. The starting point is to get the name of the public transport providers in your area so you can find them in the telephone book. In New South Wales, people should contact Country Link and City Rail for transport information. A service in Victoria puts you in contact with someone who will discuss where you want to go, timetables and costs, and a suitable route for you.

You will also be able to find out the times a low-level bus operates on particular routes. Low-level buses have an adjustable step so that people who cannot usually board because of the high step, can have the bus lowered for them by the driver. It is called a 'kneeling bus' and usually displays a sign labelling it as such.

It is also well worth while contacting the government department responsible for transport in your state. You may need to check the proper title of the department by ringing general government information, as it is not necessarily useful to look under 'T' for transport. For example, in Victoria you need to look under 'I' for Department of Infrastructure in the government listings. Once you have the correct source for information, there are all sorts of concessions and services available for older people. These include off-peak concessions, pensioners' and benefit recipients' and seniors' concessions, and an annual free trip for pensioners. It is really worth wising up on what is available through public transport for your older parents.

People using sit-on scooters or wheelchairs can ask their rehabilitation service, community health centre, or disability information service, about how to organise for a ramp to help them get on and off a train. Some stations require the person to book ahead, while at others the train driver has the ramp in the cabin and will put it in place as required.

Taxis

A Multi Purpose Taxi Card entitles the holder to half-price taxi fares and is available for older people whose physical limitations prevent them boarding public transport. Application forms are available from local government offices or the person's doctor who needs to provide medical details to support the application, prior to your lodging the application for approval. The application form provides lodgement and completion details.

Community transport

Older people may require assistance with transport if they no longer drive or do not wish or are unable to use public transport. Some community groups have volunteer transport services that will pick up an older person from home to take them shopping or to a day centre.

Depending on the state, community transport is often provided by local government or community groups. This community transport usually involves a small bus, which runs to a timetable and has a regular route with distinctively marked bus stops. The driver is a paid worker and should understand the needs of older frail people. Community buses are often equipped with a hydraulic lift, which is used to help people board. Transport on a community bus can be free, but may involve a small set charge or a donation. Another aspect of community transport is that some local governments make the bus available for self-drive by community groups during the times the bus is not on its scheduled runs, for example at weekends. This can be a great opportunity for group outings.

Across Australia there are a few areas where an organisation has been set up to maximise the use of all government-funded buses and cars available to non-profit organisations, as well as all the other public and private transport in an area. By cataloguing all resources and mapping routes, duplication can be minimised and sharing of resources can take place. Sometimes these community transport organisations are the single point of call for local transport inquiries and bookings, with the resources and volunteer drivers from a range of organisations being pooled.

For more information about your local community transport options, contact your local HACC services, local government or shire office or volunteer organisation.

Rehabilitation services

Rehabilitation services assist older people to recover from sickness, surgery or injury, by providing therapy and treatment. The purpose of rehabilitation for older people is:

- to assist the older person to recover from their illness or surgery
- to optimise their ability to perform daily life tasks and other activities
- to prevent further loss of abilities
- to minimise any increase in a pre-existing disability
- to assist them to resume their usual way of life
- to help them to access everyday activities in their community
- to minimise the long-term health care needs of the person.

Conditions or circumstances common to older people which often require and benefit from rehabilitation include:

- stroke
- Parkinson's disease
- arthritis
- visual impairment

- cardiac and respiratory conditions
- hip replacements or joint replacements
- chronic pain
- road accidents
- accidents around the home.

Rehabilitation is available to older patients in public and private hospitals and older people living at home. It is provided by:

- community rehabilitation centres (state and Common-wealth)
- day therapy centres (public)
- outpatient services attached to hospitals
- community health centres
- private practitioners
- rehabilitation in the home.

The thing that sets rehabilitation apart from some other services, is that it usually involves an interdisciplinary team (health professionals from different disciplines) working together to improve the patient's situation. The involvement of different health professionals will be appropriate depending on the trauma or disability. But whatever the composition of the team, they should work in cooperation to achieve a common agreed goal for the patient. The treatment will be time-limited and proceed according to a plan. As rehabilitation often requires lifestyle changes, the plan and consultations should include partners and other family members, especially the cook and 'social secretary'!

Rehabilitation is provided by a team of health professionals, the make-up of which will depend on the needs of the older person. Rehabilitation teams often include:

- nurses, to help older people to manage their health and provide information and advice
- occupational therapists, to help older people to undertake daily tasks and suggest aids or equipment

- physiotherapists, to work with older people to ensure they have maximum physical function and movement, and suggest physical exercise or activities
- social workers, to help with obtaining appropriate benefits, and to assist older people and their families to adjust to losses caused by their illness or accident
- speech pathologists, to work with older people to overcome or manage speech disorders or eating and swallowing problems
- consultant physicians in rehabilitation medicine and geriatric medical specialists
- dietitians to help with weight gain or weight loss, depending on whether stress has to be reduced on joints or a person needs to be built up to aid recovery, as well as to provide advice on how to prepare specially textured foods, if required
- recreation and fitness officers, who work with older people to encourage exercise and provide aids to participate in exercise or sport, such as modified golf clubs or an artificial bowling 'arm'.

Depending on the nature of the event that necessitates rehabilitation, there could be a host of other specialists involved, such as a clinical psychologist, a neuro-psychologist and a prosthetist. If your parent is receiving this specialist attention, you must decide who is overseeing the total care (possibly the doctor or a surgeon) and ask that person about the role of the various professionals and the aim of the various treatments. This will help you to judge whether treatment is going according to plan or not, and when to ask for a medical consultation to sort things out.

For government-subsidised services, there is usually a fee for a treatment which can be in the vicinity of $10 with a 'cap' if a person has to attend four or five times a week. A 'cap' means that even if the older person attends multiple times in a week, their total bill will not exceed a set ceiling. The main thing is to ask before you start. As with all

government-subsidised services, someone in the organisation has authority to waive or reduce fees in cases of
genuine financial hardship, either because of low income
or because the overall cost of treatment is causing hardship
even temporarily.

For further information, contact your hospital, or ask
your doctor for local public rehabilitation service contact
details.

Vision and hearing

Sight and hearing loss are common in older people and
can make everyday tasks and communication frustrating
and difficult. There are agencies providing vital services for
vision-impaired people in all states under a variety of
names, often run by non-profit organisations. Services are
likely to include:

- training and support for people who have little or no
  vision, to overcome fear and live independently (such as
  by being able to cross the road, walk without falling,
  catch a bus)
- home visits to advise and put in place aids to assist in
  everyday life
- a library of braille and talking books for information and
  pleasure
- low-vision clinics that help people to make the most of
  their remaining vision
- nursing homes dedicated to caring for people with
  vision and hearing loss
- telephone links to other people for discussions
- volunteers to telephone and check on isolated frail aged
  people and offer friendly visiting
- counselling
- referrals for aids and support services
- assistance to modify and continue with sport or
  recreational activities
- groups with other people with similar difficulties for
  support and encouragement

- news information whereby volunteers read newspapers on to a computer each day and people can ring in and listen.

Quite often, an organisation providing services for people with low vision will extend their service to cover sensory loss in general, thus including those with hearing loss. An equally extensive range of services is usually offered for people with hearing loss, but geared to their needs. Ask your doctor about these services in your area.

Falls prevention programs

Falls are common in all older people, even those who are healthy. They can result in broken hips, pelvis, kneecaps, ankles, nose, hands and fingers as well as in grazes, bruises and a big fright and loss of confidence. Many older people finish up in hospital as a result of a fall, which usually occurs around the home.

Most falls happen when the person trips on an uneven surface, such as a crack in a driveway, a rug, a step, the curb, an object, an uneven floor, on a wet or slippery area, because of sun in their eyes, because of glare or poor lighting, or when bending down or turning around.

These falls can then lead to an ongoing series of health problems and disabilities, which can affect the person's long-term health and well-being. Hence, the need for programs designed to prevent falls before they actually happen. This is done by visiting the older person's home and assessing the home and garden environment for risk factors and making recommendations to increase safety. To prevent falls, refer to the list of dot points provided in Chapter 4.

Falls are not the result of ageing itself and can certainly be minimised if you help your parents to stay as healthy and alert as possible.

For further information contact your state health department, HACC contact number, the Department of

Veterans Affairs HomeFront program, or local community health service.

Carer support

The term 'carer' is used to describe anyone who provides care for a relative or friend on a regular basis without being paid. Carers can be any age and do not have to live with the person they are caring for.

Because carers play such an important role for many older people, and because being a carer can become stressful and exhausting, it has been recognised that carers themselves need some support. In some services, when the older person is being assessed, the carer will also be offered a separate 'carer's assessment' that looks specifically at their needs and provides suggestions to make it easier for them to continue in their caring role.

If the older person is living with their carer, who may be their partner or another family member, it can be especially important for the carer to have a break. Short-term breaks for carers and the older person are provided through services known as 'respite care' which are described earlier in this chapter. This means that the older person is looked after by someone else, for anything from a few hours to several weeks, while the carer has a break. This may be in the older person's own home, in a day centre, or in a residential facility.

Carer support services offer:

- information and advice to carers
- education programs for carers
- brochures and booklets
- self-help and support groups for carers
- phone lines where carers can talk with health workers who understand the pressures they are under and provide moral support and encouragement
- counselling.

Carer resource centres, respite centres and Carelink

Carer resource centres have been set up to provide assistance to people who are caring for others. Caring for older people can be a challenging and stressful task. Carer resource centres are run by the Carers Association in each capital city and provide information, support, education and counselling. They can assist you with information for new carers, financial advice, arranging breaks, meeting other carers and getting help at home.

Carer respite centres are located around Australia and provide advice, support and information about respite care available in your local area. They help carers plan care and assist them to have a break by using respite care services.

Commonwealth Carelink centres are located around Australia and can put you in touch with and provide information about community, residential and aged care services.

There are no charges for these information and advisory services for carers.

Personal alarms

Many middle-aged people worry about their older parents, particularly if they are quite elderly and frail or living alone. They are concerned that their parents may fall or become ill and be unable to get help.

Personal alarms worn by the older person are like a small pendant, with a button to press if they need help. The personal alarm is connected to a computerised monitoring service (a bit like a home security system) so that if the button is pressed, the alert is raised and help sent.

The usual practice is for the monitoring service to first contact the people the older person has nominated, and if they are not available, then help is sent. These services often rely on family, friends and neighbours to visit immediately the person who has triggered the alarm. These people must be able to enter the home without the assistance of the older person.

Personal alarms can also be used to check on the older person each day. The monitoring service simply telephones the older person on a daily basis to make sure they are well. This is particularly reassuring for families who live a long way from their elderly parent or relative and want the comfort of knowing that there is regular monitoring.

There are some public personal alarm services, accessible through Aged Care Assessment Teams, which are available to frail elderly people assessed as being in need. However there may be waiting periods for these. Contact your local Aged Care Assessment Team for information.

There are also privately run services. The cost will vary significantly depending on whether it is a private or public service. Public services have minimal costs, ranging from nil to $300 per year; private services range from approximately $400 to $800 per year. First-year costs may be greater due to purchase and installation of the devices, with subsequent years being less costly. Some services may also charge for call-out if the monitoring station is required to send a staff member to check on the person.

Help for people with dementia

Dementia affects a person's memory, intellect (thinking), language, behaviour, personality and emotions. There are many different causes of dementia, the most common being Alzheimer's disease. Dementia can happen to anybody but it is more common in older persons. It affects about one in fifteen people aged over 65 years, rising to about one in every four people aged over 85 years.

Dementia is not a normal part of ageing and it is important that any concerns about dementia are investigated, to rule out other conditions and to ensure that treatment and other assistance are received. Understanding the disease and just what can be done, as well as early planning, will make a positive difference to managing living with dementia. Because people with dementia may become incapable of making good decisions, the person affected may need to consider appointing a guardian or arranging an appropriate power of attorney, while they are still able to do so (see Chapter 4).

People with dementia, and those caring for them, can use the general services listed in this chapter. There are also services specifically to cater for people with dementia, like residential care facilities such as nursing homes and hostels, and day programs that will provide care and activities. Most people with dementia remain living in the community for many years and day programs, home support and respite become increasingly important forms of assistance.

The Alzheimer's Association is an important first and ongoing point of contact and assistance. Their helpline provides information, advice and referral. They also run courses and groups for people in the early stages of the disease, as well as programs for families and carers. Support groups, telephone support, counselling, libraries and resources such as help sheets are readily available.

Help for people with arthritis

Many older people suffer from arthritis. There are almost 150 different forms of arthritis, and one of the most common is osteoarthritis, caused by wear and tear on joint linings and the breakdown of protective cartilage covering the ends of bones and joints. Most people develop some degree of osteoarthritis as they get older. Treatment includes anti-inflammatory medication, physiotherapy, exercise, rest and self-management courses. The big trend in the management of arthritis is self-management: teaching the older person strategies to assist in managing and minimising the effect of arthritis and associated pain and stiffness. Evaluation has shown that participants experience less pain and depression and are able to better manage their arthritis.

The Arthritis Foundation is a national body, with offices in each state that provide:

- a telephone advisory service
- library and resource centres open to the public
- public speakers to address community groups
- arthritis self-help courses to enable people to acquire the skills and knowledge to manage their arthritis
- osteoporosis courses that assist people to prevent or minimise the condition
- chronic illness self-management courses for people with one or more ongoing condition such as arthritis, heart or lung disease, diabetes or stroke
- water exercise programs
- self-help and social groups
- volunteer activities.

The Arthritis Foundation has branches in each state and territory. Check the telephone book for the number then telephone and ask them to send out information.

Help for people with diabetes

Diabetes effects over half a million Australians and half of these people don't know they have it. It is expected that the prevalence of diabetes will double in the next ten to fifteen years. Diabetes can effect people's daily routine and quality of life. As yet there is no cure, but research seeking a cure is being undertaken. There are ways to make living with diabetes more manageable. Healthcare professionals, such as a diabetes educator, dietitian, podiatrist, pharmacist and your parents' general practitioner, can offer support, education and information. Diabetes Australia offers support to diabetics and their families, and can assist in accessing a federal scheme for the supply of insulin syringes and diabetes testing strips.

Diabetes Australia has branches in each state and territory. Check the telephone book for the number.

Help for veterans and war widows

The Department of Veterans Affairs funds and provides a number of programs for returned veterans and their dependents. Veterans aged over 70 are assessed for a 'white card' (specific medical conditions) or 'gold card' (all conditions) which gives them access to a range of free or subsidised services.

These services include:

- aids and equipment
- doctors
- ambulance transport
- dental services
- hearing services and aids
- hospital services
- medical services
- optometry
- community nursing
- pharmaceuticals

- physiotherapy
- podiatry
- chiropractic
- osteopathy
- rehabilitation
- up to 21 days convalescence care in a residential setting (such as a hostel or supported accommodation that provides assistance with dressing, showers, meals and general support) for recuperation following discharge from hospital
- extra respite care
- transport or the cost of transport in some circumstances.

In addition to these subsidised health services, there are a range of other subsidies and concessions, including (depending on eligibility) telephone allowance, travel expenses and funeral benefits. Day clubs in some states provide support for isolated people or those at risk of becoming housebound.

The HomeFront program is designed to prevent falls and accidents in the older person's home. A home assessor, who is often an occupational therapist, visits to undertake an assessment of the home and garden environment. They look for potential hazards such as cluttered walkways and work areas, wet or slippery floors, unsafe steps or rails, loose floor coverings, and poor lighting that could cause accidents or injury. After the assessment they can provide a tradesperson to carry out minor modifications and safety improvements, and this work may be subsidised by the Department of Veterans Affairs.

The department's Home Maintenance Program provides a database of local tradespeople. The Department's Home Maintenance Helpline offers property maintenance advice and can make referrals to local tradespeople. The Department of Veterans Affairs also has a new Home Care Program (similar to those listed earlier in this chapter) which subsidises support and care to the person in their own home.

Financial help for older people and their carers

Concessions

The government provides a range of concessions for older people. These will depend on the state you live in and you will need to contact the Concessions Unit in the relevant state government department. Concessions that older people may be eligible for include:

- winter energy
- municipal rates concessions
- public transport concessions.

Concession cards entitle the holder to concessions on a range of goods and services.

There are three types of concession cards issued by Centrelink:

- pensioner concession card — inquiries 13 23 00
- health care card — inquiries 13 27 17
- Commonwealth seniors health card — inquiries 13 23 00.

A pensioner concession card entitles the holder to a range of benefits from government departments and from business.

A low-income health care card is issued through Centrelink to people who do not receive a pension but whose average income is below certain limits. Concessions include prescription medications, ambulance cover, subsidised dental and optometrist services, car registration, winter gas and electricity, and water and sewerage charges. Concessions may vary from state to state, and the card is valid for six months.

A Commonwealth seniors health card is issued through Centrelink or the Department of Veterans Affairs, to retirees of pension age who are not in receipt of a pension and whose assets are in excess of the pension cut-off point, but whose taxable income is below certain income limits. Cardholders are entitled to a concession on prescription medications listed under the Pharmaceutical Benefits Scheme.

Another concession card is the seniors card. Seniors cardholders can receive discounts from a range of businesses and travel outlets. Concessions vary from state to state, and governments publish a directory (or several, such as central, metropolitan and rural) that lists the retail and tourism organisations that offer discounts.

Discounts may apply to:

- airline travel, such as senior flyers' fares
- purchases from participating retailers and motels
- travel within states but not necessarily interstate
- entertainment such as concerts or theatres
- sports.

Benefits

The Carers Payment is available to people who provide full-time care for a frail older dependent person. You cannot receive a carer payment as well as the aged pension. It is worth noting that recipients of the Carers Payment are able to work, train or study for up to 20 hours per week and can have a respite care break of up to 63 days per year.

The Carers Allowance is available for live-in carers of frail aged people who provide a lot of additional care, who are unable to work because of their caring responsibilities and who do not get any other income support payment. Recipients can continue to get a Carers Allowance for 63 days per year if the elderly person they care for is in respite care as well as for 63 days if they are in hospital. Carers Allowance is free of income and assets tests, is not taxable, and can be paid in addition to the Carers Payment. Claim forms are available from Centrelink Customer Service Centres.

Financial assistance is also available for veterans, war widows and dependents through the Department of Veterans Affairs — refer to 'Help for veterans', above.

Palliative care for the terminally ill

'Palliative care' is the term used to describe the care that does not have as its focus the curing of an illness. Palliative care services provide for people who have terminal illnesses or who may die soon. They aim to improve the quality of life of those people and their families by providing a range of nursing, counselling and other support programs both within the person's own home and within medical or hospice facilities. Programs are provided by doctors, nurses and social workers, all of whom have specialist training in palliative care.

For older people, palliative care services offer:

- specialist medical advice by consultant physicians
- home nursing
- social worker support
- counselling for the older person and other family members
- bereavement care and support groups
- support workers
- respite care
- specialised equipment
- volunteers to assist with household jobs and tasks
- complementary therapies such as relaxation, massage and meditation
- hospice care and accommodation.

For information about your local palliative care services, contact Palliative Care Australia.

Other useful organisations

Council on the Ageing

This is a national body with offices in each state. Services may vary from state to state, but may include:

- information on residential care options
- free legal and taxation advice
- counselling
- information on a range of subjects
- insurance: health, travel, house and contents, and motor vehicle.

Libraries

- provide learning activities for older people, such as accessing the internet
- have large print books
- offer visiting library services for homebound people.

Condition-specific organisations

There are also support organisations for specific illnesses and chronic (ongoing) conditions. These organisations typically undertake research, provide information and educational sessions, and organise self-help and support groups for people with the condition. Your doctor will be able to advise you of relevant organisations or you can contact the aged care information line or check in the telephone book.

Examples of these include:

- the MS Society, for people with multiple sclerosis
- Diabetes Australia, for people with diabetes
- the Heart Foundation
- the Anti Cancer Council and cancer support groups
- the Muscular Dystrophy Association
- the Australian Lung Foundation, for people with respiratory disease
- the National Brain Foundation, for people who have suffered stroke.

Private services

There are, of course, many private services available to assist older people.

Live-in help

Full-time live-in help is not available through the public system but is available privately. A range of private agencies will provide full-time live-in carers. If you are paying for a lot of different private services, sometimes full-time live-in help can be more cost-effective.

Some families, with the financial resources, successfully arrange for care of very dependent parents in their own homes by employing 3 x 8-hour shifts of carers through the private enterprise system.

Another form of live-in help can be a younger person living with an older person, rent-free, in exchange for some help. Your parent or you could arrange this yourself as others have done over the years.

A scheme called Homeshare, successful in England, America and several European countries, has recently reached Australia. Homeshare brings together older householders, who could benefit from help in the home and from companionship, with people who are prepared to lend a hand in return for free accommodation. It is a shared housing arrangement based on the barter system, whereby the householder provides a bedroom and shares facilities, and the homesharer provides up to ten hours a week of practical assistance as well as the security of someone sleeping in the home. A written agreement is developed between parties to ensure roles are clear. The scheme currently exists in New South Wales and Victoria, and interest in setting up the scheme has been shown by other states.

Information

Having read this book, you will realise that there are thousands of organisations across Australia that provide services to older people, and that it is not possible to list them all in this publication.

You will need to be prepared to make a number of phone calls to find out the names and contact numbers for your local services. You can:

- ring the Commonwealth Government office in your state, particularly about Aged Care Assessment Teams or residential care
- ring the state government department that covers health, particularly about support services in the older person's home
- contact your local government or shire
- ring the numbers listed in the previous chapters
- ring the numbers listed under each state for particular service types.

When making your inquiries remember:

- that it will probably take you several phone calls to find the number for your local service
- to start a file and keep a record of your contacts, otherwise it can become confusing
- that individual services don't always know about other services but you can make the best use of them by asking questions such as 'Do you know of any other local services that provide a service such as…?' 'Could I have their contact number, please?'
- if they use jargon, a phrase, term or abbreviation that you do not understand, ask them to explain it.

By now you will have realised what an enormous health and community support sector we have for older people. It's no mean task finding out about all the different services and who does what. Individual services can provide information about their own services, and usually some other local services, but possibly not everything you need to know. There are some services whose job it is specifically to provide information about all the different services available.

Information services

Some services specialise in providing information to the general public about a range of issues including health services.

These include:

- Carelink Centres: the Commonwealth Government is establishing Carelink Centres across Australia in 2001. The role of these centres is to provide information and advice about community residential and aged care services. Check the telephone book for your nearest Carelink Centre or call 1800 052 222
- Citizens Advice Bureaus or Community Information Services are community-based organisations that provide free information and advice about services, financial and legal issues
- local libraries often have a display area with pamphlets of the local social and community services in the area
- local councils often publish booklets which outline facilities and services available to residents
- some state government departments publish directories of health services
- some peak organisations, such as Aged and Community Services Australia, publish directories of aged care services.

There are also many internet sites that list health services. State governments have sites which outline the government-subsidised services available. As these are updated and improved over the coming years, they will

include databases of services so that you can search for the
sort of service you want in your preferred location.

Key contact numbers

Australian Capital Territory

ACT Community Care	02 6205 5111
ACT Community Health Care Program	02 6205 2600
Aged Care Assessment Teams ACT	1800 020 102
Aged Services Association of NSW and ACT	02 9799 0900
Commonwealth Department of Health and Aged Care	1800 020 102
Community Advocate	02 6207 0707
Community Information and Referral Service	02 6248 7988
Guardianship and Management of Property	02 6257 8461
Home and Community Care (HACC) — Contact the State Department HACC Program for information about government and non-government providers	02 6205 1526
Hospice Palliative Care Society	02 6205 1555
Independent Living Centre	02 6205 1900
State Department of Health and Community Care ACT	02 6205 5111

New South Wales

Aged Care Assessment Teams New South Wales	02 9367 6811
Aged Services Association of NSW and ACT	02 9799 0900
Ageing and Disability State Department New South Wales	02 9367 6811
Combined Pensioners and Superannuants Association Information Line	02 9281 3588 or 1800 451 488
Commonwealth Department of Health and Aged Care	1800 048 998 or 02 9263 3555
Homeshare NSW	02 9599 2273
Home and Community Care (HACC)	02 9367 6811
Local Community Services Association	02 9211 3644
New South Wales Continence Promotion Centre	02 9630 0477
Office of the Public Guardian	02 9265 3184
Palliative Care Association	02 9334 1891

Northern Territory

Adult Guardianship Office	08 8999 2609
Aged Care Assessment Teams Northern Territory	1800 019 122 or 08 8973 8511

Aged and Community Services	08 8364 1180
Australian Red Cross Home Care	08 8945 3588
Casuarina Public Library	08 8927 2280
Commonwealth Department of Health and Aged Care	1800 019 122 or 08 89463444
Anglicare Top End Respite Services	08 8985 0000
Home and Community Care (HACC) — Northern Territory Health Services	08 8973 8511
Hospice and Palliative Care Association	08 8922 7004
Northern Territory Carers Association	1800 242 636 or 08 8947 3877
Volunteer Friendship Support Program	08 8948 0962

Queensland

Adult Guardianship Office	07 3234 0870
Aged Care Assessment Teams North Queensland	1800 019 030 or 07 4727 0217
Aged Care Assessment Teams Queensland	1800 177 099
Aged and Community Services	07 3870 8622
Australian Pensioners and Superannuants League	07 3844 5878
Brisbane Citizens Advice Bureau:	07 3403 5648
Commonwealth Department of Health and Aged Care North Queensland	1800 019 030 or 07 4727 2297
Commonwealth Department of Health and Aged Care Queensland	1800 177 099
Home and Community Care (HACC) — Contact the State Health HACC Program for information about government and non government service providers	07 3234 0340
Palliative Care Association	07 3832 3522
Public Trustees Queensland	07 3213 9213
Queensland State Health Department	07 3234 0111

South Australia

Aged Care Assessment Teams South Australia	1800 188 098 or 08 8237 8111
Aged and Community Services	08 8364 1180
Australian Retired Persons Association	08 8267 5711
Citizens Advice Bureau	08 8212 4070
Commonwealth Department of Health and Aged Care South Australia	1800 188 098
Department of Family and Youth Services South Australia	08 8226 7000

Guardianship and Administration Board	08 8368 5600
Home and Community Care (HACC) — Contact the State Office of the Ageing for information about government and non government service providers	08 8226 7027
Office of the Public Advocate	08 8269 7575
Palliative Care Council	08 8291 4137
Public Trustee	08 8226 9301

Tasmania

Aged and Community Services Tasmania	03 6229 1344
Aged Care Assessment Teams Tasmania	1800 005 119 or 03 6211 1411
Carers Association of Tasmania Inc	1800 242 636
Citizens Advice Bureau	03 6245 8671
Commonwealth Department of Health and Aged Care Tasmania	1800 005 119 or 136247 or 03 6221 1411
Community Equipment Scheme	03 6222 7226
Community Nutrition Unit	03 6222 7222
Community Occupational Therapy Service	03 6222 7280
Community Palliative Care Service	03 6224 2515
Community Physiotherapy	03 6222 7280
Continence Service	03 6222 7303
Council on the Ageing Tasmania Inc	03 6228 1897
Department of Health and Community Services Tasmania	03 6233 8011
Falls Prevention Resource Centre	03 6222 7280
Guardianship and Administration Board	03 6233 3085
Home and Community Care (HACC): Aged and Disability Care Information Service (ADCIS)	1800 806 656 or 03 6222 7312
Hospice and Palliative Care	03 6224 3808
Independent Living Centre	03 6334 5899
Public Trustee	03 6233 7598
Tasmania Pensioners Union	03 6234 8526

Victoria

Aged Care Assessment Teams Victoria	1800 133 374
Combined Pensioners and Superannuants Association	03 9662 3971
Commonwealth Department of Health and Aged Care Victoria	03 9285 8888
Carers Association of Victoria	1800 242 636

Community Information Victoria	03 9670 1233
Guardianship and Administration Board	03 9628 9911
Home and Community Care (HACC) — Contact your local Council, Shire or Community Health Service for information	
Homeshare Victoria	03 9530 4666
Older Persons Action Centre	03 9650 4709
Office of the Public Advocate	03 9603 9500
Palliative Care Victoria	03 9662 9644
State Trustees of Victoria	03 9667 6444
Victorian Association of Health and Extended Care	03 9820 0888
Victorian Continence Resource Centre	03 9816 8266
Victorian State Department of Human Services	03 9616 7777

Western Australia

Aged Care Assessment Teams Western Australia	1800 500 853
Aged and Community Services	08 9443 8233
Citizens Advice Bureau	08 9221 5711
Commonwealth Department of Health and Aged Care Western Australia	08 9346 5111
Continence Foundation of Western Australia	1800 814 925
HACC — Contact the central HACC Unit for information about government and non-government service providers	08 9222 4134
Office of the Public Advocate	08 9278 7300
Palliative Care	08 9420 7211
Western Australia State Department of Health	08 9222 4222

General

Aged and Community Services Australia	03 9686 3460
Alzheimers Association Helpline	1800 639 331
Carer Resource Centres	1800 242 636
Carer Respite Centres national toll free number	1800 059 059
Centrelink General Enquiries	13 23 00
Commonwealth Carelink Centres	1800 052 222
Commonwealth Department of Health and Aged Care — Aged Care Hotline	1800 500 853
Council on the Ageing (COTA)	03 9820 2655
Dementia Helpline	1800 639 331
Department of Veterans Affairs	13 32 54

Diabetes Australia	1800 640 862 or 03 9654 8777
Federation of Ethnic Communities Council of Australia	02 6282 5755
National Continence Helpline, Continence Foundation of Australia	1800 33 00 66
Palliative Care Australia	02 6232 4433

Help for people worrying about their older parents

While most help is geared towards the older person themselves, carer support services provide help and advice to people who are actively caring for an older person as well as anyone else interested in finding out about services available.

Our advice for people worrying about their older parents and investigating services on their behalf is to:

- be proactive: find out about the help and services available before the older person actually needs them
- encourage your ageing parents to do as much planning ahead as possible
- be prepared for changing relationships with your parents
- be prepared for your parents to reject your help or deny that they need assistance
- allow plenty of time. Finding out about services is very time consuming and not something you want to rush through because this will just add to your overall stress levels
- try not to get frustrated if it feels like you are going round in circles when you are trying to find out about or organise services
- contact the office of the local member of State or Federal Parliament in your parents' area if you cannot find out about the required services. The staff are usually a great source of information or will find the information for you

- talk to other immediate and extended family members and have a plan about who will be responsible for doing what. Share the load around
- decide whether to let your employer know you have ageing parents and that you may need some flexible time should they require your assistance
- take preventative steps to stay fit and healthy and not to feel guilty
- look after yourself!

Help is on the way — but 'no way' say your parents

Some families will experience the dilemma of having ageing parents unable to care properly for themselves but definitely refusing all assistance. In extreme cases, the house may be so derelict and the old people so ill cared for that neighbours may have registered complaints with local authorities or police. If your parents are in this situation, and you have tried everything you can to assist them but have been unsuccessful, then maybe all you can do is:

- maintain your contact and support as much as they will allow
- wait for a crisis and be prepared to act promptly to get assistance in place
- involve your parents' doctor and nurses at the local community health centre or Aged Care Assessment Team
- involve health professionals
- work closely with these health professionals to try to achieve a solution or improvement
- find comfort and support for yourself in this difficult situation.

Summary and checklist of services

What the older person needs	Service name	Who provides it
Help with housework	Home care or home help	Government-subsidised HACC services such as local government, church organisations, community groups and the private sector
Help with the garden or lawns	Home or property maintenance	Government-subsidised HACC services such as local government, church organisations, community groups and the private sector
More social activity	Senior Citizens Clubs; day activity services; social clubs; friendly visiting	Government-subsidised HACC services such as local government, church organisations, community groups and private companies; community groups; volunteer services
Better food or help with meals	Home-delivered meals; group meals	Meals-on-wheels; private delivered meals; day centres; Senior Citizens Clubs
A change in routine or a break	Respite care; carer support	Home care; respite care centres; residential services
Help recovering from an operation, illness or injury	Rehabilitation; allied health professionals including physiotherapists, occupational therapists, speech therapists, nurses	Hospitals; extended care centres; convalescent care; community health centres; private practitioners; community nursing
Home and personal safety	Falls prevention programs; community policing programs; personal alarms service	HomeFront; HACC home maintenance and home modification; Aged Care Assessment Teams; private alarms; community police
Getting to and from places	Community transport	Volunteer organisations; community groups
Help with personal care or health issues	Personal care; allied health nursing	HACC personal care; HACC and community nursing services; Community Health centres

7 Questions you should ask

Questions you shouldn't be afraid to ask,
understanding the lingo and getting what
you want

How often do we hang up the phone and then think, 'I wish I'd asked...'

Because it's often hard to think of everything you should ask in advance, this chapter has gathered up some questions from throughout the book as well as listed new ones for you to consider.

When seeking assistance for your parents, you may be dealing with people providing a service as well as health professionals offering advice on options for treatment. Because the type of questions will differ depending on which of these situations you are in, questions are listed under the two main headings of 'Questions to ask service providers' and 'Questions to ask health and medical professionals'. Within each of these are subsections that deal with both general questions and questions specific to different types of services.

Obviously you will not wish to ask all the questions listed here. In fact, many questions will be answered if on your first enquiry you ask the service to send a brochure or any written information. You may like to mark the questions you want to ask before you make the phone call, or prepare your own list of questions with space to note down the answers you are given.

Questions to ask service providers

Fees and charges

- How much will it cost?
- If charges are on a sliding scale, what is the basis for this decision?
- Does someone have authority to completely waive fees in case of financial hardship, and who is that person and what is the basis for such a decision?
- How will my parents be billed and by what method can they pay?
- Can accounts be sent to another person, such as another family member or a trustee?
- What happens if an account is disputed by my parents?
- Do my parents sign an agreement to pay?
- Are there any penalties for late payment?
- Are part-payments over an extended time possible?
- Are there different rates for after-office hours or weekend service delivery?
- Are there any charges other than an hourly rate?
- Is there a minimum charge and if so, what is it?
- Do cancellation fees or other types of penalties apply to a failed service, or non-attendance by my parent or the worker?

Insurance

- Are your workers fully covered for any injury they may suffer at my parent's home, whatever the cause?
- Do you have a policy to reimburse or make recompense in cases of dishonesty, or for lost or broken valuables?
- Do my parents need special insurance of any kind in regard to your workers caring for them either in their home or at another venue (such as a day centre)?
- Are my parents covered against accidents that may occur while being transported to your service, or in the car of one of your workers?

Staff

- How many staff do you have?
- Do you have male and female workers, and can my parent choose the worker's gender especially for personal care?
- Do you have workers who can speak my parents' language?
- What qualifications or training do your staff have?
- How much experience with older people and in this particular task does your staff have?
- How much are staff supervised?
- Are staff aware of their obligations in regard to confidentiality of my parents' situation?
- How do you ensure that staff practice your requirements regarding confidentiality?
- How are staff vetted for honesty and integrity, for example do they have a police check prior to employment?
- When you employ new staff, do you check referees?
- What would you do if my parents did not like the staff member providing the service?

What if?

What would you do if your staff member:

- did not like my parents?
- did not think my parents were entitled to the service?
- thought my parents' house was too dirty or untidy, or too opulent, to receive the service?
- thought one of my parents could do more to help?
- thought my parents should pay to go 'private'?
- thought I should help instead?

Service standards

- Is your type of service required to be accredited (reach a certain minimum standard to be allowed to operate)?
- If so, has your service attained accreditation?
- Does your service have written policies to cover complaints, standard of work and confidentiality?
- Is there a waiting list, and if so how are priorities determined and managed?
- Are there any circumstances in which you would withdraw the service from my parents and refuse to provide that service?
- What rights would my parents have to try to reverse a decision to totally or partially withdraw services?
- What is the attitude of your service in regard to interested, close relatives and next-of-kin?

Emergencies

- What sort of situations would your service/staff regard as an emergency if they were providing a service for my parents?
- What training do your staff have to deal with such emergencies?
- What would your staff do in an emergency concerning my parents?

- Are all your staff equipped with mobile phones?
- Do your staff have access to a senior person for advice at all times while working with older people?
- How do you ensure that a specified relative/friend/neighbour of my parents will be notified in case of an emergency with my parents?

Communication and changes

Will my parents be provided with written information about whom to ring:

- with queries about the service, the account, or the worker?
- to request to change the time of a service or a worker or a task?
- to cancel a service because parent is unwell or has another appointment?
- about how much notice is required to alter or cancel a service and not incur a fee?
- about how much notice your service can provide if there is a change to service, or worker, or task?
- for lodging a complaint?

Can I arrange for you to notify me also of changes to my parents' service, any change in their health or ability to cope, or of any new service they take up on your advice?

Records

- What sort of information will you be asking my parents to provide (eg. detailed medical history, personal life details, financial position)?
- What documented evidence will you require in regard to my parents' financial position?
- How will this information be recorded (such as electronically, on paper)?
- Where will you keep the record of all the information?

- What security have you to keep these records safe (such as from general view, from loss)?
- Who will be able to read these records?
- Do you share the information in your records with any other service and if so under what circumstances and by what authority?

Complaints

- Does your service have a documented complaints procedure?
- If so, will my parents get a copy of this document?
- Can you give me a brief description of the complaints process?
- How promptly are complaints dealt with?
- If my parents complained about a worker, would the service stop immediately and only restart after the complaint had been dealt with?
- If my parents complained about a worker but could not manage without your service, what would you do?

Home care, home help and housekeeping

- Will my parent have to provide a vacuum cleaner and all cleaning materials?
- Do you have a list of preferred, or banned, cleaning products, to give my parents?
- What if my parents cannot afford the cleaning products you stipulate?
- If my parents' vacuum cleaner is old and not working very well, can your worker bring one?
- If my parents want the oven cleaned instead of the shower on a particular day, without extending the length of time, can they make that change just by asking the worker to do it?
- If not, how can small changes to the tasks be made by my parents?

- How can bigger changes to the tasks done, or the time allowed, be made?
- Will your worker clean the house if my parents are not at home (eg. because they are at a medical appointment)?
- Do my parents have to supply tea or coffee for your worker's tea break?
- How long would a worker need to be at my parents' house to be entitled to a tea break?
- Will my parents be linked to the HACC 24-hour emergency service because of receiving a service from you?
- Can you explain the HACC 24-hour emergency service to me?
- Who will explain the HACC 24-hour emergency service to my parents?

Property and home and garden maintenance

- Would the maintenance person bring all necessary tools, washers, batteries, globes and the like to replace those worn out?
- Would my parents pay the worker for these things or would the items go onto their account to be paid in the usual way?
- What if the worker broke something while at my parents' home?
- What would happen if the work was commenced but the worker could not complete it for any reason, thus causing inconvenience for my parents?
- What redress would my parents have if they did not like the finished job?
- If the maintenance job was small, such as replacing a few globes, would my parents have to pay for a minimum amount of time?
- If so, what would that be, and could they choose to ask the worker to do a few other things to fill in that amount of time while they were at the house?

Delivered meals

- Can the meals be delivered either hot or cold?
- If delivered hot, does that mean that the meals have just been freshly cooked, or are all the meals pre-cooked and frozen then reheated prior to delivery?
- At what time would the meal be delivered?
- My parent does not have a microwave oven, will the meal heat satisfactorily in an ordinary oven or will there be loss of nutrition?
- Would the meal be left if my parent is not at home?
- What if my parent cannot get to the door to take delivery?
- What happens at weekends and public holidays?
- Does my parent have a menu to choose from, or does your service only record dislikes not to be sent?
- How would my parent order a special diet (such as diabetic sugar-free, non-fat, no dairy products, kosher, or vitamised)?
- My parents have a very limited range of food that they eat. How would you cope with that?

Home health care, nursing, personal care

- Will the same worker attend my parent each time?
- Can my parent stipulate a male or female worker?
- Who provides dressings and ointments? If the nurse or personal carer, how will my parent be billed for these items?
- Does your service have a maximum number of services that you would provide in any one week (such as only three showers a week)?
- Who decides if a nurse should do the task or if a personal carer should do it?
- Would a nurse ring my parents' doctor if concerned about their health, or report to a nursing supervisor, and would that person ring the next of kin recorded in my parents' file or my parents' doctor?
- Would a personal carer ring my parents' doctor if concerned about their health or would the carer report to the supervisor of the service? Would that person contact the doctor or the person recorded as next of kin, or what would be done?

Questions to ask health and medical professionals

Fees and charges

- Will this service be bulk-billed or will my parents need to claim this account from Medicare?
- How much above the schedule fee will your fee be?
- Could my parents request a longer consultation and what would the fee for that be?
- As my parents have private health insurance 'extras' cover, can you tell me how to describe the service you are offering so that I can find out if their insurance will cover part of the fee?

- Will you provide my parents with an account or is payment of the fee due at consultation?
- Do you charge for missed appointments?

Emergencies

- What procedure do you follow if my parents have a medical or other emergency at your premises?

Communication and changes

- How will you communicate with my parents in regard to their treatment, condition, options, any changes in the situation, or changes to personnel treating them?
- In what circumstances will you also communicate with me so that I can be involved in decisions and kept informed of changes to services?

Multiple service providers

When more than one health professional is treating your parent, you need to ask:

- Who has the 'lead' role?
- Who should be contacted in an emergency relating to the current treatment?
- Who should be contacted in regard to a lack of progress, regression or change in regard to the current treatment (eg. if they are feeling unwell or if they experience a deterioration after they return home from hospital), their surgeon or their local doctor?
- What should my parents do if feeling unwell, late at night? Should they ring the hospital where they had their operation or treatment, their surgeon, an ambulance, or their doctor?

In addition

You may have more questions you would want to ask. The main points are:

- Know who to contact if you or your parents are concerned about some aspect of their treatment, health or the service they are receiving.
- Keep in touch with services if your parent is not coping with the amount of service or is dissatisfied.
- Contact the service or health professional for a review of the situation if you or your parent think their situation is deteriorating or changing.

8 Don't panic — what to do when unexpected things happen

Dealing with the unexpected, emergencies and coming home from hospital

Events big and small are happening in our lives all the time, no matter what our age or occupation or interests, and dealing with ageing parents is part of this richness of life. In the future you will be living and dealing with your own old age! This of course is not to suggest that dealing with the dramas of ageing parents is 'as easy as falling off a log', which by the way is to be avoided, especially if you are getting on in years!

Don't panic

The motto 'Don't panic' is appropriate for any unexpected event or emergency. It is a good approach to adopt and develop throughout your whole life and not just when you are confronted with problems that arise with your ageing parents. A cool head and calm approach will mean you can still think about the problem and weigh up different courses of action to eventually find a solution. But most importantly, if you don't panic you can support your parents who may no longer have the physical, mental and emotional resources and endurance they once possessed. They may feel very vulnerable in the face of the problem, be it an unexpected fall, kitchen fire, lost purse, house break-in or serious ill health.

Understanding

It is also important to keep things in perspective; we can all lose things, forget appointments or burn the dinner. This is annoying for us and others, but we are all human and we all need support, comfort, care and love throughout our lives, including in old age, and especially when things go wrong. A lecture from you to your ageing parents, on how not to do things or how silly they are, will not address the problem. What they need to hear from you is that you understand how distressing it was for them and that you will assist them in putting things right, if needed. They need to be reassured that you care about them and that they are not a nuisance.

It could be time though for you to take a hard look at your parents, their needs, their capabilities and their total environment, and to actively step in to prevent panic and disasters, large or small from happening. It may be time to organise an assessment and some services that could ease the pressures your ageing parents may be feeling, but may not be recognising or don't want to recognise! No one wants to get old but there is tremendous value in the motto 'Enjoy the age you are'. So help your parents to achieve this by taking practical action that will support them, and you will minimise panic all around.

The amount of your time spent supporting parents both practically and emotionally needs to be addressed by you and your immediate family, partner and children, and your brothers and sisters. If ageing parents or their situation demand more time and energy than you have to give at a particular time, for a range of reasons, this will cause you to feel guilty, stressed, irritated or angry.

As discussed in earlier chapters, talk to your family members and share out the tasks and the support role. You may also find it helpful to keep in touch with each other more, to give each other support while you in turn support your parents. Over time you may find your own situation changes and you can give more or less time to your ageing parents, due to things like changed employment or home address, health problems, or the needs of your own children or other dependants.

Be prepared

Part of the knack of coping successfully with ageing parents is to put the motto, 'Be prepared' with 'Don't panic'. It can be helpful to be aware that your ageing parents will in general most likely not remember immediate or recent things as well as they used to, their eyesight and hearing will be poorer and their physical stability or coordination not as steady and quick as it was. So it follows that certain events may occur. You can ponder these facts and possibilities and prepare yourself without worrying yourself or your parents. Take another look at Chapter 3 and think about your parents and their ageing.

Knowing some of the unplanned incidences that can happen with ageing parents is a help, because you can be prepared and may be less shocked yourself.

——————— *Story* ———————

A COUPLE OF YEARS *ago, Judith was at work when she received a telephone call from a total stranger to say her mother had just had a very bad fall in the street. The ambulance had arrived but her mother would not go in it to hospital. Judith quickly untangled herself from work and drove to the location. She found her mother in a state of shock and very bloody but very sure that she did not want to go to hospital. After an unhurried physical examination, calm questioning and discussion with the ambulance staff, Judith drove her mother home where she could rest, recover and get her own doctor to check her.*

Judith was glad that she did not panic, which could easily have happened as her mother looked so injured and bloody. It would have been easy for Judith to insist that her mother go to hospital, especially as her face was cut and messy and she has osteoporosis and a history of falls and fractures. Judith reminded herself that older people commonly experience falls, and stayed calm and listened to her mother's wishes, her answers to questions about how she felt and especially listened to her mother saying that she could move without pain. Judith thought about other options, like taking her mother to hospital later, or taking her to her doctor's surgery. But, Judith did as her mother asked. She took her home and stayed with her until she had recovered from the shock. Judith contacted her mother's doctor who came to the house and checked her out. Listening and acting according to her mother's wishes was definitely the right decision, because in this case Judith's mother needed the dentist not a hospital!

Prevention

Falls are a major risk for your ageing parents, not only outdoors but in their own home. Their home is where they are likely to have the most common accidents. Although falls are not a normal part of the ageing process, as people age they may have medical conditions or be on medication that may increase the risk of having a fall. It is important for you to anticipate some of the situations in your parents' home and take action with your parents to prevent falls and other accidents from happening and to ease your own mind. It is recommended that you take time to ensure your ageing parents' home is as safe and secure as it can be. There are loads of simple things that can be done that will prevent a panicky situation later. Take a look at each room of your parents' home and take the necessary precautions — refer to the important points raised in Chapter 4.

Accepting help and support services

When the time has come for your parents to have services to help maintain them at home, things can go awry sometimes, but don't panic. If your parents are very critical of the way a worker is cleaning the house, it may mean the new cleaning service is not up to scratch, or this may simply be a way of your parents making a statement that they are still adjusting to the changes of ageing and need time to settle in with the services. If you think it will help, you can look at what is not acceptable to your parents with the cleaning and sort out what they want done and convey this to the cleaning service. If the tasks are clarified and all carried out, this is a good start. Some cleaning services do not include washing windows, for example. You may then be able to pay extra or organise another service that does this cleaning, if this is what your parents want done.

Things can get a little more serious when older parents do not want services although they want to stay at home. Your parents may not be strong enough or fit enough to do all that is needed around the home or to maintain their personal care and well-being. You may be even more concerned if your mother or father lives alone.

Sabotage

Some ageing parents definitely sabotage the best laid plans about which you may have consulted them and all of which they have agreed to. Your parents may have agreed to phone one of the services themselves to organise their involvement. After one or two weeks of the plan being in place, you may check how the various services are going only to learn that your parents have done such things as:

- complained about the standard of the cleaning and refused to have the cleaners back
- complained that the meals were awful and left them in the freezer not eaten
- failed to contact the supermarket
- cancelled the day program without ever giving it a go!

However, on a more successful note, you may learn that the personal care worker is coming to shower the parent who is too unstable to manage independently and whom your other parent is too frail to help any longer.

Don't panic if sabotage occurs. You need to look again at how your parents are coping and reassess the situation. You may want to talk things over with the main service provider and obtain their advice and assessment of your parents' situation. It is clear that your parents have accepted the need for the personal care worker to help with the showering, so this has occurred. This is good news. As your parents do not want the delivered meals, suggest that they do not have them every day but order for three or four days a week only. Then when your parents are too tired to cook, they can take one of the meals out of the freezer.

Ask why your parents haven't organised for the shopping to be delivered and perhaps do that yourself. It may be that they have not got around to it, or it is hard for them to accept that they can no longer just get in the car and drive to their favourite shops. Don't push the day program until they are used to the other services or are interested to go themselves. It may be that they would rather stay at home and enjoy outings with the family every now and then.

See how it goes

The amount of service being provided to your parents in their home may not be ideal according to your standards, but your parents may feel comfortable with less rather than more help. Leave it and see how they manage. Whatever the reasons for rejecting services, rational or irrational, don't panic. It may take a couple of tries at organising services or it may take more gradual introduction of services over time. It is very important for your ageing parents to feel the services are of value to them even though you might feel better if all the services were in place at the outset. Keep an eye on how the services are going and encourage your parents to accept them. You will have to make it clear, for example, that you cannot be there all the time for them when they want something down the street. Watch out for sabotage and be practical and supportive of your parents.

Forgetfulness

Forgetting things is another hazard of ageing, one for which you need to keep your cool. Don't panic if you arrive at 10 am to take your parents to one of their numerous medical appointments for 10.30 am and they are still having their breakfast, have not showered and have forgotten all about it. Ring the doctor's surgery to see if they can be seen at a later time or make an appointment for another day. Forgetting an appointment will be distressing for your parents, especially if they like to be reliable and punctual and are aware that they are now forgetting things that they once found simple to organise and remember. Keep calm and be kind to your parents. Develop a new approach for appointments. You could phone them about the appointment the night before or even the same morning and tell them the time you will be over to pick them up.

Misplacing things

It is also common for some ageing parents to misplace things such as credit cards, accounts, keys, appointment cards and so on. The short-term memory can be affected by ageing, with more recent events the ones that can elude recall; older people finish up forgetting where they have left things, or spending a lot of time looking for things, or both! If you receive an urgent phone call from your parent saying they have lost their credit card, do not join their panic. Instead talk things over on the phone, such as:

- where they have looked
- where they have visited today and may have left it
- when and where they remember seeing it last
- when was the last time it was used.

If you live nearby you may be able to visit your parents and make a search with them. Sometimes things are found in their right place and it is more that the older person feels so worried and agitated that they cannot look properly, or their eyesight is poor and they fail to see it in a wallet, bag or drawer. If it is not practical to help with the search, then you will need to cancel the credit card and organise a new one. Resist cancelling the card altogether just because you feel it may be lost again. Credit card insurance may be an option to reduce anxiety for you and your parents. As we know, credit cards are very useful and safer for older people than carrying around wallets or purses full of money.

Lost house key

A rather frightening experience for your ageing parents is to be locked out of their house. This is particularly distressing if your parent lives alone and you are not close by to provide quick assistance. Talk over this potential crisis in advance with your ageing parents and have an agreed plan that your parents are happy with and will remember. If your parents do not have a plan, they may be able to use a neighbour's phone to call you and you can then provide them with reassurance and a solution. If you want to be prepared for this happening, organise a spare key to be held by a friendly and trustworthy neighbour who is home during the day. Your parents can very easily go next door and receive help or just pick up the spare key. If your parents are too independent to accept this arrangement or they don't have such a neighbour, then they can plant a key outside the house but away from the front door area, for security. Another solution is for your parent to wear a personal alarm, which they can press for help. Or if their house key is small and light, they can wear it on a chain around their neck.

Fire

Just the idea of your ageing parents having a fire in their home can make you feel quite panicky. Again, taking steps to prevent this is essential for your parents' safety and your own peace of mind. You will no doubt have thought about fire safety in your own home, so along with utilising those ideas check your parents' home to ensure that:

- all electrical cords are unfrayed and in good condition throughout
- power points are not overloaded
- smoke detectors are installed near the bedrooms
- smoke detector batteries are tested regularly and replaced as necessary
- the area where your parents cook is uncluttered, well lit and generally safe
- heaters are regularly serviced
- open fires have spark screens, and the chimneys are regularly swept
- safe arrangements are made for drying clothes (a clothes horse near an open fire or unguarded flame or element radiator can be a hazard)
- electric elements on radiators are screened.

You may also like to consider whether your parents could operate a fire extinguisher and at least show them how to use a fire blanket. Have these items installed in the kitchen, as the most likely cause of a fire is a mishap in cooking. A personal alarm which can be pressed requesting help may be something you also want to consider.

We all hope that a fire will never occur but these precautions will certainly help, as will the development of a fire plan which could include some of the following aspects:

- Leave keys in the doors that have deadlocks so that the key is in place should your parents need to get out in a hurry.
- Designate a place outside, away from the house, where your parent should go to if there is a fire.
- Keep a hose connected to a tap close to the house.
- Encourage your parents always to take action if the smoke alarm goes off.
- Go over with them what to do if the smoke alarm goes off, for example, when there is a false alarm caused by burning toast, a small fire, or the potential for a large fire.
- Have the fire and other emergency numbers printed on the phone in large letters.
- Have a fallback position if your parents' phone may be too close to the fire, for example, go to neighbours to call the fire brigade.
- Impress upon your parents to leave the house and get help, rather than try to rescue all their possessions.
- Ensure that some treasured possessions, for example photographs, are easily removable.

If your ageing parents have had a house fire they will need lots of support and love to help them through the awful experience, their memory of it, and their fear of it occurring again. Even a small fire in the house is frightening for anyone. Don't join the panic. Check how the fire started and how your parents dealt with it. Go over and improve the fire plan if necessary and try to ensure that any potential fire hazards are rectified. Your parents may feel reassured if they see steps have been made to help prevent the situation re-occurring.

Of course, you will also need to help your ageing parents clean up their house because there will be a mess, and some items will be damaged by fire, smoke or water. Many items in the house may be blackened and foul-smelling. Help your parents check their insurance policy, which may be able to assist with some of the costs of repairs and replacements.

Break-ins

A house break-in is another crisis that may confront your parents, not because they are ageing but because break-ins are relatively common. They are likely to feel very troubled if this occurs, so don't panic, as your parents will need you to remain calm. It is normal for people to feel angry and unsettled when their house is broken into, but older people already feel vulnerable and this type of incident can really accentuate this feeling.

Supporting your parents and remaining calm and taking action on the break-in will be a great comfort to them. You are likely to be the first person they phone when they realise their house has been burgled or damaged, so it is vital for you to you speak calmly and sensitively with them. They may not be able to explain the details clearly at first, so be patient. Arrange to go to their home as soon as possible, as your physical presence will be reassuring for them. You may need to direct your parents on their next steps or phone the police yourself. Inform your parents that the police will make a home visit.

To help prevent further break-ins, to keep your parents safe and to keep your feelings of panic in check, assess the security of your parents' home. This needs to be done in a non-dramatic way so your parents do not feel unduly worried and insecure. There are many simple and in-expensive ways to ensure that your ageing parents' home is secure, even if they are away on holidays. The following steps will encourage or help them:

- Don't leave messages on the front door.
- Don't leave the front door key under the mat.
- Don't use address tags on keys.
- Don't arrange a home delivery when nobody will be home.
- Don't have an overflowing letter box.
- Don't let strangers into the home unless sure of their identity.
- Install external sensor lights which are activated by movement.
- Report broken street lights immediately.
- Display their street number clearly.
- Keep side gates and garage doors locked.
- Notify insurance company, police and neighbours when they will be away for extended periods.
- Mark valuables so they can be easily identified.
- Install a peep viewer and a security door and do not open the door to strangers.
- Prune outside bushes and creepers to eliminate hiding places.
- Make sure windows and doors are secure at all times.
- Close curtains and blinds at night when lights are turned on.
- Be very cautious of unsolicited tradespeople who tell them that their home needs repairs.
- Deposit valuables in a bank or other secure place.
- For holidays, cancel regular deliveries such as the newspaper.
- For holidays, ask neighbours with a second car to park it in their driveway.
- If away, ask neighbours to collect their postal mail and to clear junk mail from the box.
- If away, use timers to create a normal light pattern and to operate a radio.
- If away, leave blinds in their normal position.

Be calm

These are some of the common incidents that you and your ageing parents may face, but with awareness of their possibility, some early practical action and a prevention approach, your ageing parents will be in a more safe and secure situation. They will also benefit from your calmness and steady support, which you are more likely to offer if you are prepared.

A health crisis

Other crisis situations you need to prepare for with ageing parents are health related. The same principles apply: don't panic and be prepared. Inform yourself of some of the common health crises that may occur with your parents and be familiar with the more obvious physical symptoms they may experience. With your parents' agreement you may want to attend some of their medical appointments to learn about their medical condition, their medication and just to make contact with their doctors. Your parents may also give permission for you to further inform yourself and phone the doctor privately to obtain extra information on possible health implications that may arise and when. Getting your parents authority sooner rather than later is a good idea.

Keep key contact numbers at your fingertips, such as your parents' general practitioner, specialist doctors, ambulance and nearest neighbour. This will help you respond in a crisis and reduce your panic response. It is natural to feel very concerned if your ageing parents are not well. You may even feel helpless, but you can prepare in advance so that you can play your part in helping your parents as well as possible should you get an emergency call.

If, on the other hand, your ageing parents are still active and decide to go travelling interstate or overseas, don't panic. They may not experience any problems and if they do, there are usually a variety of ways to develop a solution! Adequate health and travel insurance is essential for peace of mind and as a resource in solving problems away from home.

Other health crises can unexpectedly happen right here at home. It is important to stay calm and act quickly in these circumstances. Take stock, think about who you need for assistance and contact them urgently. Refer to those key contact numbers you have listed in advance and take action. Once you have reached your parents, listen to them but also take charge. Be firm but kind and considerate. Explain why certain things must be done which will maximise the help your parent requires.

—————— *Story* ——————

*M*AVIS WAS PLEASED SOME *years ago when her widowed elderly older sister, Betty, took a three-month holiday overseas. It was her sister's first overseas trip and a great opportunity. She was to accompany some close friends who included the tour guide. Betty had always wanted to travel but had felt this was unlikely now that her husband had died. However, here was her chance and being older would not stop her. For two months Betty had a wonderful time. Then while alone in London on a relaxed shopping trip, she tripped and fell on a shop step that was half in shadow. The shop manager phoned an ambulance and off she went to an unknown hospital with an unknown injury. A short time later Mavis got a phone call from the hospital breaking the news. Time to panic? No. At the time Mavis did not want to spend the money she had saved for a different purpose, on an airfare to London. Mavis had some guilty feelings about not being willing to rush to her sister's side. But she stayed calm and decided to help her sister through this crisis from a distance.*

Betty required hip surgery and was in a London hospital for six weeks! Mavis followed up her travel insurance, which covered the health costs, and people from Betty's tour group rallied around. Mavis sent letters and flowers to cheer her up. Mavis also ensured plans were made between her travel insurance company and the hospital for her flight from London to Melbourne.

Throughout this situation, Betty needed support and a positive attitude from her sister, Mavis. She certainly did not want panic, or worry and agitation. Mavis really provided wonderful support. Betty recovered extremely well and met some lovely people during her time in hospital!

_____ *Story* _____

*R*ECENTLY ONE SUNDAY MORNING, *Barry collapsed. Without warning as he attempted to walk to the bathroom, he fell down, hitting the bedside table and knocking the lamp as he went. He came around from the blackout after fifteen minutes and struggled to phone his daughter Kate. Even though Barry had his phone by his bed it was on the other side from where he fell. Finally with enormous effort Barry got to the phone and called Kate who received the desperate SOS from her Dad. It was hard for Kate to make out the whole story but obviously she needed to reach her Dad quickly. Had Kate lived further away she would have called an ambulance immediately, but as she lived just fifteen minutes away she decided to go to her Dad's aid. Before leaving her own house, Kate telephoned her Dad's doctor asking him to make a house call to her father as soon as possible as he had met with an accident at home.*

Barry needed practical assistance and reassurance. Having a doctor check him out was essential and this was done. Providing calm support was critical as Barry had just experienced a very frightening event. Kate and one of Barry's older grandchildren stayed with him in shifts to cover the 24 hours for a few days, by which time he recovered sufficiently to manage with his usual home care services.

This type of response is good if the medical opinion supports it, your parent is not wanting to go to hospital, and there is family or a carer able to live in to monitor and provide adequate support to the unwell ageing parent.

Going to hospital

Going to hospital is not really complicated but it helps to know what is involved. Make sure your parent takes all their current medication with them to hospital to show to the nursing staff and admitting doctor. It is best if you can accompany your parent for support and to read any documents they may be asked to sign, such as authorisation for medical procedures which go beyond those discussed prior to admission. This is a big step and your ageing parent needs to hear a simple but positive explanation as to why this needs to happen. Sometimes it is a relief for ageing people to go into hospital but others are fearful, so you need to provide them with support, comfort and sometimes a distraction so they are not totally focussed on their health crisis. You can do this by telling them about a happy recent event with one of their grandchildren or a light-hearted news item you just heard that would interest them.

Ambulance needed

If it is an emergency then an ambulance can be called. Upon arrival at the home or incident, the ambulance officers will ask what has happened, check out the patient and may administer, for example, pain relief medication or oxygen. They will then take the patient to the nearest available hospital emergency department. Some ageing parents like to have a case packed for this type of emergency.

If you possibly can, accompany your parent to the hospital, making sure your family is informed of what is happening and organise for someone to come and keep your other parent company if necessary. It is good if another family member or close friend can meet you at the hospital, so you too can have emotional support and have someone to talk to about any decisions regarding your ageing parent's treatment.

If you cannot go to the hospital, see if another family member can, but if not just ring ahead and ensure that the hospital knows who you are, how to contact you and that you want to be kept informed.

A non-emergency ambulance trip may be arranged for your parent if a doctor has organised it. While you may be willing to drive your mother or father to hospital, you may find you cannot manage to walk them to the car, that they cannot bend to get into the car, or that they are in too much discomfort to sit in the car, so an ambulance is appropriate. A doctor will need to arrange for the ambulance.

A trip in an ambulance is costly. It is wise to check either that your parents are covered by their pension or benefit for the cost of an ambulance or that they pay an annual subscription to the appropriate ambulance service in your state. If your parents have private health cover, it may be that their fund reimburses the cost of the ambulance subscription or at least the cost of an emergency trip. Either way you really should ensure that your parents have ambulance cover of some kind.

Home from hospital

When it comes time for leaving hospital, it may not be as easy as you imagined! But don't panic. If you don't think your parent is ready to go home yet, you need to consider other alternatives for where your mother or father can stay for a few weeks. Your ageing parent may have had a heart attack or surgery, for example, and now have recovered enough from that acute condition to leave hospital. However this does not necessarily mean that they can just pick up the pieces and get on with their life at home as it was before. Your ageing parent is likely to:

- tire easily
- have lost general physical condition from being in bed in hospital
- be more easily confused
- be less able mentally and emotionally to assess, plan, organise and manage their changed life situation.

They may have been seriously ill and fully cared for in a protected environment where decisions have mostly been made for them, and personal care and catering fully provided. You need to assess your parents' abilities now compared to their abilities before their health crisis.

If your parent lives alone, consider whether they will be able to care for themselves. If living with your other parent, a partner or a friend, consider whether that person will be up to the job of looking after your convalescing parent.

Coming home from hospital successfully requires good planning from all those involved, including you. You can develop a checklist for your parent's discharge including:

- date of discharge. Ask to be informed of this as soon as possible after the decision has been made, so as to help in arranging assistance at home.
- recovery and special instructions. Ask how long recovery may take. Ask how should your parent care for themselves. Ask whether there will be any restrictions on your parent's activities.
- a hospital summary of your parent's treatment and their next appointment date. Give this to your parent's local doctor.
- sufficient medication, or prescriptions for enough medication, to last until your parent can visit their local doctor. Make sure that your parent understands what the medication is for, and how and when they should take it.
- transport home. Will your parent be able to get into a car or will they have special transport requirements?
- any support services or equipment that they may need on their return home.

Not all hospitals are competent at planning for aged patients when it comes time to leave hospital. Many medical specialists concentrate on their particular area of expertise in relation to patients, including the aged patient, and do not look at the bigger picture. For example a cardiac specialist will address a cardiac condition but when this is under control, either through surgery or medication, the specialist will not necessarily consider other life aspects of the aged patient or refer them to a geriatrician for an aged care assessment.

If you have doubts about how your ageing and unwell parent will cope alone at home, or how your other parent will cope with the demands of their increased caring role, you can request to have your parent seen and assessed by a geriatrician or the hospital social worker, while still in hospital. An aged care assessment can be organised to look at all aspects of your parents' situation and to arrange convalescent or respite care at another facility if this is needed. When your parent does return home, services such as house cleaning, delivered meals, home nursing, personal care, personal alarm, rails and ramps may be needed. Further down the track some respite care may be needed for the carer, or for your parent if they live alone and are getting tired through self-caring.

Taking stock

After any crisis or health trauma, once the professionals have made their assessments and given advice, services have been put into place for your parents, and your parents have had a little time to settle back at home, you really need to 'take stock' of your parents' new situation yourself. It can be useful to look at this in terms of:

- managing daily life at home
- managing their affairs
- your parents' emotional state and mental health
- benefit from further assessment, for example by a geriatrician
- your parents receiving appropriate medical treatment for their condition, or for their comfort, for example because of pain
- care by the most suitable services
- granting power of attorney to someone if your parents are no longer able to manage their financial affairs or make other life decisions
- making an appropriate will

- considering other residential options if appropriate at this stage.

Reference to previous chapters in this book may be helpful now, as most of the above situations have already been covered. As part of your 'taking stock' it may be time to go through some of the checklists again in regard to your parents' ability to manage and the family resources available to help.

Medication

Taking a range of medication is part and parcel of the older person's lifestyle these days, with many taking tablets for a number of conditions such as heart failure, high blood pressure, arthritis and diabetes. Your ageing parent may in the past have remembered to take their medication but may now have become less reliable. They may begin to panic if they cannot recall whether they have already taken their tablets, and as no one else knows their 'system' there is no way of checking what has been taken. If they phone you and ask what to do, this is no time for you to panic. Your parent or you can phone the doctor or pharmacist and obtain their advice on what tablets your parent should take immediately, or what other action they should take. Then there needs to be discussion between the pharmacist and your parent on how best to manage the tablets in the future.

Dosette boxes are an excellent way to overcome these dramas. Most pharmacists will fill a week's supply of tablets in a dosette box for little or no cost and some will deliver this to the older person's home each week. The tablets are placed in a section in the box marked for a particular day and for a particular time of day. Stay calm and help your ageing parent adjust to the dosette box system. It is very reliable if used correctly and you can tell if a dose of tablets has been taken just by looking at the container.

Terminal illness

When your ageing parent is confronted with a terminal illness, you will need to offer support and encouragement. Naturally you will be upset and it will take time to adjust to this knowledge. It is helpful to talk over the situation with the doctor, both with your parent there and also privately to prepare yourself for future events and your parent's health changes. Treatment options will need to be evaluated and many ageing parents will want others, including family members, to listen to what they want. Don't panic if your parent wants to undergo aggressive treatment or on the other hand refuses treatment altogether. Listen to their wishes. Try to understand why they have made their choice. There are a range of services you may want to follow up, such as cancer support groups, palliative care services, hospices and nursing homes.

If your ageing ill parent wants to plan and discuss their funeral arrangements with you, this can be very helpful for all concerned. Once again it is important to listen to your parent's wishes and reassure them that you will carry them out if this is what they want. Chapter 11 discusses in depth the death of a parent. If you cannot cope with the discussion, find someone in the family or a friend who can listen to and record your parents' wishes.

Your own response

Now you are more aware of the crises, both minor and major, that you may encounter with your ageing parents, you need to assess your own situation and stress tolerance. There are a number of pointers and strategies provided here for you, but you need to know yourself and how you react to pressure and a crisis. If you are not trained professionally in this area, or are not used to handling crisis, or have a nervous disposition or are finding the whole thing with ageing parents too much, then you can consider a couple of other options.

Support for you

If your parent receives some support from services already, you can talk to the service providers about having a case manager allocated to your ageing parent to coordinate and review your parent's service needs and to follow up how the services are going. If you are able to get a case manager, you will find much less call on your time and your frustration with organising things which keep 'falling apart' will be greatly reduced.

Another alternative is to consider a short course in stress management at your local neighbourhood house, community centre, TAFE or University of the Third Age. This will be an advantage to you in all areas of your life, not just when you are supporting your ageing parents.

You also need to assess the support you yourself are receiving when you are helping out your ageing parents and assisting to resolve their dramas. As you are also ageing, you will not have endless physical and emotional reserves for demands of children, house, garden, parents, friends, work, recreation, community work and so on.

It helps to fill in all the family on what is happening with your ageing parents. Usually there is something each family member can do, even a small thing like an occasional phone call to their grandparent to say hello. These contributions can all help to support you and your ageing parents.

If you feel alone in this role or unsupported, take action and involve others, whether family, friends or services. This will help you out when a crisis occurs. You are less likely to panic if you feel you are connected to your own system of comfort, reassurance and support at a time when things are difficult or not under control with your ageing parents.

At all times keep your sense of humour as there is nothing like a good laugh to release tension and keep life in perspective. And remember, 'No one gets out of here alive'.

9 Simple solutions to everyday problems

The run-down on equipment, gadgets and home adaptations

MUM, THE RUBBER GRIPPING DEVICE IS FOR OPENING JARS ...NOT REPRIMANDING DAD!

GOLDING

There is an amazing array of aids and equipment designed to assist older people and people with disabilities to do everyday tasks and activities. This chapter provides information about some of the most commonly used aids and equipment so you can consider whether they might be helpful to your older parent. In many instances it is good to have an occupational therapist provide advice on whether a particular aid will be suitable for your parent and recommend where to get the item.

In addition to using aids or equipment, your older parents may need to make small alterations to the design or layout of their home, such as installing a ramp or widening a doorway to allow a wheelchair through, to make everyday living easier. Contact your local community health service or equivalent to seek the advice of an occupational therapist before spending money on renovations or equipment which may not be suitable for your parents' needs or ability.

In the kitchen

Older people can lose strength and dexterity in their hands and arms, making it more difficult to grasp utensils, open jars, chop food and generally function as easily in the kitchen and around the home as they have in the past. This problem can be alleviated easily with the help of useful everyday devices.

There are simple and inexpensive gadgets available to help older people, such as:

- for opening jars: a simple rubber gripping device which allows for easy opening of jars with tight lids and which requires less strength and grip
- for turning on taps: a simple plastic handle that fits over normal tap handles and provides easier turning and more leverage to turn taps on and off tightly
- wands that are easier and safer to manage than matches to assist lighting the gas or fires
- gadgets and grips to assist in lifting pots and pans
- specially designed sharp knives for chopping foods, for people with weaker muscle strength or reduced ability for fine movement in their arms, hands or fingers
- easy wheel trolleys to move items around the kitchen without having to carry them
- cutlery grips which are rubber grips that slide over the handle of cutlery and make it easier to hold
- teapot pourers that allow tea to be poured out of the pot without having to physically lift the pot from the bench or table.

In the bathroom

The bathroom is an area where safety can easily be compromised because of small spaces and slippery surfaces. Items to assist in the bathroom include:

- non-slip rubber mats in the bottom of the bath or shower
- a bath seat/bench made of wooden or plastic rails that rests across the top of the bath and allows the older person to sit on it and either get into the bath or use a hand-held shower to bathe themselves
- rails beside the toilet, bath or shower to hold onto and provide extra stability and support for people pulling themselves up or down
- shower chairs that are plastic seats with draining holes, to sit in under the shower, or that can be wheeled in and out of the shower, for frail older people who are unable to stand up
- toilet chairs for people with hip and knee problems or frail people who have trouble bending down to sit on the toilet and stand up again. These chairs are like a toilet seat in a frame which easily wheels over the toilet, and because they are higher, require much less bending
- raised toilet seats that are several inches thicker than the normal seat, to raise the height of the toilet
- commode chairs
- special non-slip vinyl for the bathroom floor and other wet areas
- hoists to lower and raise people in and out of the bath
- hand-held showers
- special power points and switches
- thermostats for keeping bath or shower water at the required, not-too-hot temperature
- continence aids such as pads, bed sheets, or special underwear.

In the bedroom

A good night's sleep makes anyone feel better. If getting in and out of bed is a challenge for the older person, or they have difficulty with aspects of dressing, consider:

- chocks to raise the bed higher off the ground so it is easier to get in and out of bed and requires less bending
- a bed stick to assist in getting out of bed
- pressure mattresses
- lights that can easily be operated while in bed
- a telephone next to the bed
- long-handled grabbers that allow the person to reach out and grasp or pick up items without bending over or having to lean over too far
- long-handled shoe horns and gadgets to help pull up socks or special stockings for people who have difficulty reaching their feet
- gadgets to assist in doing up buttons for people who have reduced dexterity and movement in their fingers
- large face clocks.

In the living room

Older people often spend a good deal of time in their favourite armchair, reading, watching television, doing crosswords, relaxing, snoozing or talking on the telephone.

There are a number of items that can make the living area more user-friendly to older people:

- chairs which: are higher than normal so the person has less distance to move to sit and stand; support the lower back; ensure the hips are slightly higher than the knees; allow the feet to rest flat on the floor; have arm rests
- electronic tilt chairs that will tilt the person forward or back to sit or stand more easily
- long-handled grabbers as for the bedroom
- remote controls: for just about everything, including the television, music system, heating and air conditioning
- portable telephones that can be placed near the person regardless of where the telephone socket is
- magnifying lamps which are like reading lamps with a large magnifying glass and allow the person to read easily
- page turners to help turn the pages of books or magazines
- big print or 'talking' books
- a sloping stand with a page clip for easy reading.

MUM, THIS REMOTE CONTROL WILL OPERATE EVERYTHING FROM THE TV TO THE HEATING... ..EXCEPTING DAD OF COURSE!

GOLDING

In the garden

Raised garden beds, which are built up off the ground, can be easier to manage as they require less bending and stretching. If this is too costly, a bench for holding pots is a good alternative. Considerations for older gardeners include:

- a combined padded kneeling bench and support frame
- long-handled garden tools, broom and dustpan set
- changing the garden gradually to be low maintenance.

Moving around: aids to mobility

There are many aids to mobility available to help older people. It is important that mobility aids are specially recommended by a professional to suit the individual involved. This usually means having a physiotherapist assess the older person and recommend the type and make of aid that is most suitable.

Aids and equipment include:

- wheelchairs
- walking sticks
- three-pronged walking sticks (these provide more stability than a single-foot stick)
- walking frames
- electric wheelchairs
- electric three-wheel sit-on scooters
- swivel passenger seats for cars: the normal front passenger seat is removed and a swivel placed underneath it, allowing the person to sit directly on the seat and then swivel the seat and their body and legs around into the car. Cheaper alternatives are also available which are placed on the top of the car seat and allow the person to swivel around
- portable fold-up ramps.

Getting aids and equipment

- You can buy small items of equipment easily from pharmacists, some community health services and other retail shops.
- You can often borrow or hire equipment from community health centres, hospitals, public rehabilitation services and organisations such as the Red Cross.
- You can buy equipment privately from rooms of health professionals and through mail order by phoning for catalogues from major suppliers listed in the telephone book.
- You can buy, sell and exchange equipment.

Independent living centres

Independent living centres (usually run by community groups) have large showrooms with a comprehensive range and hundreds of examples of aids and equipment and provide information (such as fact sheets and brochures) about the different items, brands, costs and where they can be purchased. You can visit or telephone for advice before purchasing. Remember, for any significant or expensive aids or equipment, get professional advice first. Consult the telephone book for your local centre.

Government schemes

The state government in each state has a scheme to subsidise or provide increased access to aids and equipment for frail older people with disabilities.

The scheme is called the Program of Aids for Disabled People in Victoria and it subsidises the cost of aids and equipment to assist people of any age who have permanent disabilities and restrictions. This service is not available for people who live in residential facilities such as hostels or nursing homes. People have to apply to the program and be assessed by a health professional who will make a recommendation about aids and equipment. The program has a high demand so there may be a waiting period. Aids and equipment available include:

- some wheelchairs and motorised sit-on scooters
- orthotics such as braces, callipers, special shoes
- wigs
- mammary protheses for women who have had a mastectomy
- electronic voice aids
- some continence aids
- some walking aids such as walking frames or special crutches
- personal care aids such as bath seats, specialised beds or mattresses, commodes, grab rails, hoists, over-toilet seats, ramps, raised toilet seats, shower chairs and stools
- oxygen
- pressure mattresses and cushions.

Another example is the scheme in Queensland which pays for the costs of incontinence pads for assessed pensioners.

The contact numbers for similar government aids and equipment programs in each state are:

Australian Capital Territory

ACT Equipment Services	02 6244 2222

New South Wales

Health Department Program of Appliances for Disabled People	02 9391 9472

Northern Territory

Territory Independence and Mobility Equipment Scheme	08 8922 7244

Queensland

Medical Aids Subsidy Scheme	07 3250 8555

South Australia

Disability Equipment Scheme	08 8226 6466

Tasmania

Royal Hobart Hospital	002 6388 695

Victoria

Program of Aids for Disabled People	03 9616 7777

Western Australia

Health Department	08 9222 4134

The Department of Veterans Affairs Rehabilitation Appliances program also provides a wide range of aids and appliances, including wheelchairs, walking frames, continence aids and rails.

10 Moving homes — are nursing homes the only option for later on?

The facts about supported residential care and nursing homes

Most older people live independently in their own homes. As they get older they may use many of the support services listed previously to assist them in doing tasks and remaining in the residence of their choice.

Once you have read this chapter, you will realise that perhaps some of the stories you have heard about nursing homes may in fact be about other types of residential care. So keep an open mind as you read through this chapter and absorb the range of options that are available to elderly people.

If you are concerned about your parents' ability to manage either now or in the future, don't jump to the conclusion that they will eventually need to live in a nursing home. In fact only a tiny proportion of frail aged people live in nursing homes because their needs are so great that they cannot be supported in the community.

To move or not to move?

For a range of reasons, your parents may decide, with or without your support, to move out of their traditional home into a different residence. This may be influenced by concerns about:

- their ability to cope on their own
- the state of the property
- stairs to second storey rooms or an upstairs unit or flat
- their safety
- the desire to live closer to you so you can visit them and monitor their well-being more easily
- loneliness
- poor health or illness.

Moving home at any life stage is a demanding experience. Moving for elderly people can be an even greater one. Leaving a family home can be interpreted as leaving behind memories, friends or neighbours, and acknowledging ageing and frailty. On a more positive note, it can also mean the excitement and anticipation of a new home, more contact with family and friends, and an easier lifestyle.

Many older people wait until a crisis occurs, such as the death of a partner, before they will leave the family home. This is not always the best approach. In fact many of these same older people say in retrospect that they wish they had moved earlier when their partner was still alive. This way they could have settled together into a new home that was more suitable to remain in should one partner die, and they would have shared memories together in their new home.

It may be that your older parents should consider moving into a smaller home for exactly these reasons, and you may want to be proactive in considering the options rather than waiting for some sort of crisis to occur. This will not only help to minimise the stress and anxiety involved, but ensure that your parents have ample time to think about their options and make well informed decisions.

Accommodation options

Options for older people to consider include:

- renovating their current home and adapting things there to make life easier later
- 'downsizing' to a new smaller home, apartment or unit as the larger family home and garden becomes difficult to maintain
- moving into a retirement village
- living with family members or in a granny/grandpa flat on a family member's property
- moving to serviced or supported accommodation/ residential care where some care and support is provided
- eventually moving into a government-subsidised residential facility such as a hostel or nursing home.

Each of these options is discussed below.

Renovating now to make life easier later

Some homes will lend themselves to being renovated so that they are suitable for older people. Renovations and modifications can help make the home easier to maintain, more suitable for support services to provide assistance in, and safer and more comfortable for older people. If your older parents are considering renovating or making modifications, they should seek advice from the home modification services listed in Chapter 6. This will help them and you to decide whether renovations will meet your older parents' needs for the years ahead, and whether this is the best thing to do, both for now and the future. Staying at home is not always the best decision.

If your parents are thinking about renovating to continue living at home, some points to consider are:

- whether or not the renovation will seriously over-capitalise the property
- whether or not the renovation will make the house attractive to most potential buyers in the long run
- using security doors and screens
- using security eye-viewers to identify visitors without having to open the door
- using sensor lights which come on automatically in dark areas and pathways when movement is detected
- using higher wattage globes in the house and two-way light switches in the hall and bedroom
- having portable or cordless telephones and a telephone in the bedroom within easy reach of the bed
- allowing for handrails or grab-rails beside steps and in the bathroom
- ensuring a continuous non-cracked, non-slip pathway (with hand rails) from the house to the letterbox and from the back door to the clothes line and rubbish bin
- installing a bench or shelf, or a small table or chair, near the front and back doors for placing items and parcels on
- adding power points, to avoid cords on the floor, placed high above the skirting boards to avoid bending down
- installing a wall oven with doors that slide upwards to reduce bending and reaching
- having rounded corners on bench tops and tables
- ensuring adequate cupboards and cupboard space at mid-height to avoid bending to low cupboards and reaching to high cupboards above shoulder height
- giving consideration to pull-out drawers (instead of cupboards and shelves) below bench tops, for easy access
- turning-around spaces near doors and in hallways that will easily accommodate a person in wheelchair

- installing slip-resistant flooring, especially in the bath-room and toilet
- having room for a chair for dressing and undressing in the bathroom
- having enough room in the toilet and bathroom to allow for grab rails and a wheelchair or shower chair
- ensuring maximum shower access by using a three-door slider or shower curtain
- eliminating a step into the shower
- having a level not a sloping block
- avoiding large trees and lots of climbers on fences, which mean greater maintenance needs
- minimising garden and lawn areas
- installing raised garden beds
- modifying the driveway to eliminate any difficult manoeuvres.

Downsizing to a smaller home or unit

In many cases, downsizing to a smaller home or unit will be more practical and sensible, and may also be more financially attractive than undertaking renovations or making major modifications.

Some general points for your older parents and you to consider about moving or downsizing to a smaller home or unit are:

- What location do they wish to live in?
- How easy is the access to family members, particularly those who provide support and assistance?
- How easy is the access to friends?
- Is it in walking distance (or electric sit-on scooter dis-tance) to and from shops?
- How hilly is the area? (the less hilly, generally the easier and safer)
- Is it a lonely area where most people go to work or is it an area with a lot of older people around?

- Is it near a doctor they like?
- Is it near a hospital?
- Is there public transport they can safely use if they wish to?
- What health and community support services for older people are available in the area, such as a community health service or rehabilitation hospital?
- Is there a local government subsidised service if help is needed with gardening, and access to an odd-jobs man?
- Can they get delivered meals if necessary?
- Is there a local day care centre for social activities, to share a meal, or for organised outings such as pictures, shows, musical concerts, coffee, an arts centre?
- How suitable will the home be for their future needs, for example if they need a walking frame, wheelchair or motorised sit-on scooter?
- If one of your parents died, would the surviving parent be happy there?

Living with family members or in a granny/grandpa flat

Living with family members is sometimes an option. This may mean living with the family in their home, living in an attached suite of self-contained rooms, or in a unit on the same property. The issues to consider if you are thinking about your older parents living with you at some stage in the future are covered in Chapter 2. It is an enormous commitment and will affect your lifestyle.

You may, however, find it easier to have your parents on site because of the travelling time you will save. If your parents are in a separate area from you, you can make rules about the amount of 'dropping in' or 'time together' and thus reduce the effect on your lifestyle.

Another option is movable units, often known as 'granny' (or 'grandpa') flats. These are portable self-contained units for an older person to rent and live in, that can be placed in the rear of a relative's home. Further information about them can be obtained from your state government housing department.

Retirement villages

Retirement villages are run by private management companies and also by community and church-based non-profit organisations, and must accord with the Retirement Village legislation in each state. There are several hundred villages across Australia. The occupancy type or 'tenure' varies but can include strata title ownership, leasehold (similar to rental), or licence arrangements.

Retirement villages generally offer two types of accommodation:

- self-care or independent living units/villas. These may be one-, two- or three-bedroom units with or without a garage or car space.
- serviced units/villas or apartments. These may have one or more bedrooms, with or without a garage or car space.

Most accommodation in retirement villages has a 24-hour emergency call button monitored by staff for when assistance is required. Accommodation is designed to make living and maintenance easier than in a large family home while still providing for independence, privacy and property choices such as individual gardens and garages.

Self-care or independent living units/villas are similar to a normal home or unit and are totally independent. However residents still have access to the range of communal recreation facilities and services offered. People living in self-care or independent living units/villas can still receive the range of support services listed in Chapter 6, such as home care or delivered meals, which are provided by public and community organisations.

Serviced units/villas or apartments in a retirement village are for those who wish to receive or who require support services on a regular basis, such as meals, laundry and housekeeping. Meals are provided by the village, either to the person in their unit/villa or in a communal dining room.

Retirement villages vary in terms of the services provided and the 'feel' of the place and level of interaction and joint activities offered. They might include:

- a village mini-bus to provide transport
- a recreation centre
- a village shop
- a workshop
- a craft room
- a bowling green, swimming pool and spa
- a tennis court
- a vegetable garden
- doctors' consulting rooms
- visits by allied health staff such as physiotherapists or podiatrists
- banking facilities
- a hairdresser and beautician
- on-site home help
- a library
- a club house
- boat and caravan parking areas.

A manager is responsible for the day-to-day running of the village including staffing for gardening, property maintenance and domestic help. Most retirement villages have residents' committees or regular meetings and newsletters to keep residents well informed and provide them with the opportunity to participate in decisions that affect the village community.

As with any change in accommodation, considering moving to a retirement village is a major step. You can encourage your older parents to visit a range of different villages to observe the lifestyle offered and get a feel for the characters of the various communities. During these visits you should talk to staff and residents, look at copies of the newsletter and ask for a copy of village rules and other documentation. Independent financial and legal advice is absolutely essential for anyone considering a retirement village.

Some retirement villages offer three-tier accommodation: independent living unit, hostel/supported care and nursing home care. This means the older person can avoid being moved as care needs increase or should they become more frail or ill.

The Retirement Village Association in each state (listed in the telephone book) can provide information packages and listings of retirement villages.

Supported accommodation and supported residential care

Supported residential care services offer some level of care and support to older people. They may have different names in different states, and include:

- supported residential services
- supported accommodation homes
- rest homes
- boarding houses
- private hotels
- serviced apartments.

All of these offer various levels of care and support. Supported residential services, supported accommodation homes, rest homes, boarding houses and private hotels are often in large converted houses, where the resident has a bedroom, bathroom and communal dining, meals and living areas. They are privately operated facilities which are not government subsidised, and in most states they are required to be licensed. Although the government inspects and monitors minimum standards in these facilities, because they are privately owned and operated, proprietors may decide to sell. This means that tenure in these facilities may be less secure than in other types of accommodation and people may be given short notice to move. The standard of these facilities varies enormously, as does the cost. People living in these types of accommodation are mainly independent but may require some assistance with personal care or daily tasks.

There are also serviced apartments (not meaning the ones which are part of retirement villages) where housekeeping tasks and exterior maintenance is provided.

Care packages

Community Aged Care Packages cover the provision of care to a person in their own home, equivalent to that which would be provided in a hostel if the older person had been assessed as eligible to go into a hostel (see below). The difference is that the older person remains living in their own home and the care is provided to them there. This can include assistance with bathing, dressing, meals, medication, laundry, transport, gardening and social activities. Community Aged Care Packages are provided by the Commonwealth Government as an alternative to moving into a hostel. Fees for care packages vary between about $25 and $30 per week and, if the older person is a pensioner, cannot exceed 17.5 per cent of the older person's pension.

Extended Aged Care Packages are the same, except that they provide a higher level of care to the person in their own home, equivalent to what they would be receiving if they were living in a nursing home.

Both of these packages have been introduced by the Commonwealth Government as an alternative to residential care. Because of this, people must be assessed by Aged Care Assessment Teams, who decide whether the older person is eligible, and have the responsibility for approving applications to them.

These packages really give older people more choice. After being assessed as having needs high enough to go into a hostel or nursing home, they can then choose to have the same services delivered to them in their own home. If an older person finds they cannot manage on say the Community Care Package, they could be re-assessed to see if they could receive the higher level of care under the Extended Aged Care Package. If an older person finds eventually that they cannot manage at home, then they still have the option of moving to a nursing home.

Residential care — nursing homes and hostels

Even though we often read or hear about nursing homes or hostels, only a small proportion of the aged actually live in them, so the chances are that your parents may never get there. Research has shown that, due to the frailty and illnesses of people admitted to nursing homes, they are likely to be there for less than a year before dying.

The decision that your older parent or relative needs residential care is one of the hardest decisions that you and they may ever have to make. The best approach is to consider all the factors, resources, wishes and interests of the people most affected and involved and try to make a decision that best caters for the interests of your parent and their carer.

This can be particularly difficult in a situation where one of your elderly parents is quite ill and requiring residential care, while the other is able to remain living fairly independently. Location of the residential facility is crucial in this situation. The parent still living at home can play a big role in easing the shock of the move by visiting frequently, and being present at some meal times to help feed their partner if necessary. Many older people who have been 'devoted couples' feel happy about this as it will ease the isolation and separation for one and may reduce feelings of guilt (at not being able to care for the person at home) for the other.

However, if the relationship between the older couple has been fraught with problems, the partner still living in the community may choose not to visit frequently. In this case, it may be better to find a nursing home nearer to a relative with whom the ailing elderly person has a better relationship and who may visit.

Residential care refers to living in a hostel or nursing home. The government has divided these into two different levels of care:

• Hostels, which provide accommodation and low-level care for people who need some help every day, for example with dressing, showering, medication and mobility. Hostels provide meals and some social activities. Staff are on site 24 hours per day but do not provide full-time nursing care.
• Nursing homes, which provide high-level care for people who are very dependent on others to undertake most tasks and need continual nursing care. In addition to nursing care, these facilities also provide laundry, meals and personal care such as bathing, dressing, medication and mobility. Nursing staff are available 24 hours per day.

Assessment by the local Aged Care Assessment Team (refer Chapter 5) will be needed to determine the level of care the older person requires and to authorise their entry into such a hostel or nursing home. If your older parents are recommended for placement in such a facility, the Aged Care Assessment Team worker will give you a list of places in your area to visit.

Hostels and nursing homes are heavily subsidised by the government but still require the payment of some fees and charges. These fees and charges include:

- daily care fees. This is to contribute towards the cost of the older person's daily care and the amount depends on their financial circumstances and ability to pay. The fee is based on pension rates or on the person's income. For example, a pensioner may be asked to pay up to 85 per cent of their pension for their care. The cost for part-pensioners or self-funded older people will be higher than this, but the maximum that a person can be asked to pay in daily fees is about $66 a day.
- accommodation payments. These contribute towards the cost of the residence and building and vary, based on whether the person is in a hostel or nursing home and their level of assets. For example, if the older person's assets are greater than $25,000, they may be asked to pay an accommodation charge or bond, the amount of which is negotiated with the hostel or nursing home. It is an amount agreed between the resident and the service and there is no fixed amount or formula for determining this.
- respite care fees in a hostel or nursing home, about $22 overnight.

There are also some residential facilities known as 'extra services place'. These offer residents a higher standard of accommodation and have higher charges.

Leave

Older people can take leave from a nursing home or hostel for up to 52 nights per year. While your parent is away they will have to continue paying the daily fee.

Choosing a hostel or nursing home

There have been examples in the newspapers of nursing homes that have not provided adequate care for residents. It is very difficult to judge what makes a good hostel or nursing home and where the older person will be happy and receive the best level of care. Even though all these facilities are required by law to meet certain standards, you will still find a big difference when you visit and compare them. Remember, what you are looking for is good care, not just good buildings and furnishings!

You will need to visit a number of different places with your older parent and perhaps have other family members visit to get a feel for the different places and to help you decide the ones you prefer. When you have decided which you prefer, you will need to fill in application forms and place their name on the waiting list.

You may wish to ask how many names are on the waiting list and how long the wait may be. When vacancies arise, the people who are considered to have 'priority of need' will be contacted.

It can be a difficult and stressful time having your parents waiting to be offered a place. Because the waiting lists are often very long, you may decide to move them into one place with the hope of transferring to another over time. Or you may encourage them to use respite care services (see Chapter 6) during this waiting period. Alternatively, it may be time to go back to Chapter 2 and start listing the extended family's resources to see what assistance could be raised to help tide your parents over the waiting period.

Some residential facilities combine independent living units (see retirement villages above), a hostel and nursing home on the one site, and this can be good if the older person initially requires low-level hostel care, but then progresses to needing high-level nursing home care. It means that they can 'age in place' and do not have to move to a new facility as their needs and level of care requirements increase.

People who live in hostels and nursing homes have rights. When an older person moves into such a facility, they will have to sign a contract and which sets out the terms and conditions, the fees and their rights. You may wish to get legal advice for your older parent before they sign.

To prepare for visiting hostels or nursing homes, consider the following factors and write a list of what your parents would like and other points to note.

Rooms

Consider these points:

- Does the older person need a single room, a shared room, or a room to accommodate both themselves and their partner as a married couple?
- Is there good telephone access and a telephone near the bed?
- Can the older person bring their own furniture or some of it?
- Do residents have their own pictures or photos on the wall, books and ornaments about or are the rooms all alike and impersonal?

Location and transport

Look at these factors:

- Is the nursing home or hostel located in a residential area or is it surrounded by factories?
- Is it in an area with which the older person is familiar and in which they would like to live?
- Is it near a bus, train or tram line so that people can visit easily?
- Does the service have its own mini-bus to take people out?
- Is it within walking distance of shops?
- Does the location make it easy and convenient for friends and family to visit?
- Is there car parking for visitors?

Attitude and staff

The attitude of staff is one of the most important elements to think about; it is the staff who provide the care and who help the older person to feel happy and contented. Be prepared to observe staff and the way they speak to the people who live there and to one another:

- Are there enough staff to stop, talk and listen?
- Is there a pleasant hum of activity and conversation?
- Do the staff appear friendly and relaxed?
- Do staff appear to respect the residents' wishes?
- Do the staff appear hurried and impatient?
- Do the staff greet residents, family and friends naturally and in a friendly way?
- What tone of voice do staff use when speaking with residents — is it respectful and friendly or patronising and bossy?
- Do staff appear to respect privacy and dignity — are personal care activities such as showering, toileting and bathing undertaken in private?
- Is information treated in a confidential manner?

- Are religious and cultural preferences taken into account?
- Do the staff wear uniforms so it is easy to see who is staff and who isn't?
- Are visitors welcome at all times or are there set visiting hours?
- Would family and friends be comfortable visiting here?
- What are the qualifications of staff?
- Are there registered nurses available 24 hours a day?

Food and meals

Find out:

- Can visitors stay for a meal?
- What sort of food is on the menu?
- Is there a choice of food or is it a set menu?
- Can residents participate in planning the menu?
- Are appropriate meals provided for particular cultural groups?
- Can residents be taken out for a meal at short notice?
- What is the dining area like?
- Does the food look and smell appetising?
- Can residents take as long as they like over a meal or are they rushed to finish it?
- Are meals provided at set times?
- Are snacks and drinks available at other times?

Buildings and surrounds

People have different likes when it comes to the style of building and surrounds. Studies have shown that many older people benefit if the place they move to reflects the style of the era of the furniture and even the crockery that they used in their own home. Some points to consider are:

- Does it appear attractive to your parents?
- Is it open and airy with plenty of space and natural light, or small and cosy with an old world atmosphere?

- Is there a garden with shady trees and annuals so they can mark the passing of the seasons?
- What is the level of security?
- Do the home, furnishings and garden look clean and well maintained and cared for?
- Does equipment (such as wheelchairs) look clean and well cared for?
- What is the smell when you first enter the building? Are there pleasant home-like smells such as coffee and toast, or smells more like a hospital?

Recreation and activities

Is the older person interested in recreational activities? Residents should be encouraged to pursue activities and leisure interests. When you visit, observe whether residents are involved in activities or sitting listlessly.

For example, does the service:

- offer gardening?
- offer music and singing?
- have a billiards room?
- encourage games and cards?
- organise outings?
- allow pets or have 'house pets'?
- have a library?
- have visiting hairdresser and beautician?
- have a woodwork shop?
- have outdoor areas suitable for safe, short walks, or for outdoor games such as bocce, modified croquet, or bowls?

Health care and services

Nursing homes and hostels have to comply with standards to ensure that an adequate level of care is provided for residents. You can ask the service about its policies in relation to any of the following points that are of relevance to your older parents' health:

- pain management
- skin care
- continence management
- oral and dental care
- dementia care
- behavioural management
- rehabilitation

- special feeding
- oxygen
- special medical care
- physiotherapy
- occupational therapy
- speech therapy

After the move

After the older person has moved into a hostel or nursing home, be prepared for emotional reactions from them, other family members and yourself. It is normal for you to feel a mixture of sadness, relief and guilt. Your role as a carer or supportive relative will have changed again, and like all change processes it will take some time and soul-searching to adjust. Re-reading the main points about 'feeling guilty' in Chapter 2 may be useful at this stage.

You may find visiting your parent in a hostel or nursing home difficult, even if the travel time is not greater. When they were in their own home, a visit could entail doing the odd thing about the house and talking about what they had been doing in the house or garden. But when a person is in a hostel or a nursing home, they are not doing so much for themselves so they are likely to have less to talk about. Maybe they will feel depressed, unsettled and un-communicative. All this can make the visit hard going and after about ten minutes you would really like to leave. It is helpful to take something to stimulate interest or conversation, like a photo album or a piece of hand work you are doing or that they once did, cuttings from the newspaper about things you think they may be interested in, children's drawings, report cards and the like.

You may find that when it is time to leave, your parent is feeling brighter and you are feeling very flat. It is worth persevering with visiting as it is important for anyone living in an institution of any kind to have someone showing an interest in how they are getting on. The staff often appreciate this as the relatives have an opportunity to notice the care they provide. Sometimes you can give the staff another perspective on your parent which will help in their care and heighten their appreciation of the person themselves. By visiting you can see for yourself how the staff treat and relate to your parent. There may be times when your will need to bring some matter to the attention of the manager of the facility.

Story

*I*N ANSWER TO YOUR *enquiry, yes, Auntie Jane has settled into the nursing home quite well, except for one thing. She worries the staff because she gets very agitated at meal times. Whether they bring her a tray in bed or bring her meal to the sitting or dining room she hardly eats anything and is losing weight, and you know how thin and frail she is already. I was telling that nice nurse who's there on Wednesday when I go, that Auntie Jane used to be so keen on her food having been a cook. The three of us got into a conversation about cooking and jobs, and Auntie Jane said that she used to enjoy her food more when she was working and on the run. That was about three weeks ago and you'll hardly believe it but they now let Jane have her meals in the kitchen when the meal preparation is over, but there is still activity, and she is eating and enjoying her food. They really are good there!*

Residential care rights

The following services will assist if you have concerns you wish to discuss or complaints about residential care. They may provide a support worker or advocate to assist you in making a complaint or advocating for your parents' rights.

Australian Capital Territory

Disability, Aged and Carers Advocacy Service	02 6242 5060

New South Wales

The Aged Care Rights Service	02 9281 3600 or 1800 424 079

Northern Territory

Top End Advocacy Service	08 8981 5883 or 1800 812 953

Queensland

Older Person's Advocacy Service	07 3260 6755 or 1800 818 338

South Australia

Aged Rights Advocacy Service	08 8232 5377 or 1800 802 030

Tasmania

Advocacy Tasmania	03 6224 2240 or 1800 005 131

Victoria

Residential Care Rights Residential Care Rights	03 9602 3066

Western Australia

Advocare	08 9221 8599 or 1800 655 566

Other

Commonwealth Department of Health and Aged Care — Aged Care Complaints Resolution Scheme	1800 500 853

Information

Aged and Community Services Australia is the national industry body for many community and residential aged care service providers. It has over 12,000 organisations as members providing care to over 170,000 older people. The association in each state may produce directories or magazines of aged care services or can provide advice about where to get them.

These directories or magazines usually list the different sorts of services available to help older people, including both community-based services provided in their own homes and residential services such as retirement villages or nursing homes. The services are often listed for a particular region or local government area, making it easy for you to get the contact details for the services closest to your elderly parent or you.

You can ring the relevant state association to inquire about and request a copy of their service directory or magazine. These are often provided free of charge or for a small charge to cover the cost of printing.

Aged and Community Services Australia State Associations:

Australian Capital Territory

Aged Services Association of NSW and ACT	02 9799 0900

New South Wales

Aged Services Association of NSW and ACT	02 9799 0900

Northern Territory

Aged and Community Services	08 8364 1180

Queensland

Aged and Community Services	07 3870 8622

South Australia

Aged and Community Services	08 8364 1180

Tasmania

Aged and Community Services	03 6229 1344

Victoria

Victorian Association of Health and Extended Care	03 9820 0888

Western Australia

Aged and Community Services	08 9443 8233

Other

Aged and Community Services Australia	03 9686 3460

11 Death of a parent and arranging the funeral

mum, WHY IS THE TOILET SEAT UP?

I JUST NEED TO KEEP A FEW LITTLE REMINDERS OF YOUR FATHER.

GOLDING

There will be a wide variety of circumstances in which a person will experience the death of a parent. It may mean that there is now one bereft parent to assist, or no parents left, perhaps even no relatives at all. There may be distressed relatives to support, including young adults and children, while one still has to deal with one's own feelings and life's problems. We will endeavour to cover a range of situations in the hope that there will be some useful information for everyone.

The death

The death of someone with even a serious illness can often come as a shock to the partner or other relatives, as the following story helps to illustrate.

Ten years or more ago the majority of older people would have died in hospital or an institution of some kind. Currently, with people preferring to remain in their own homes as long as possible, the number of people dying at home is increasing. Your parent may die at home. In this event you need to telephone their local doctor or the last treating doctor and ask them to call and confirm that death has taken place and organise for a death certificate to be provided.

Even if a person is in hospital, many relatives are still shocked that people die when they do. Often one hears that the relatives have all kept a vigil at the bedside for many hours or even days. The ill person may appear more restful or exhaustion takes over the relatives and they leave to get a meal or a bit of a rest and the person dies in the short time they are out.

Whatever the circumstances of a death, shock is usually experienced by relatives and friends. There are many excellent books to assist people who are grieving.

Story

I GUESS WE WERE lucky Dad died the way he did. He would have hated to be in a nursing home. Last Saturday the police came to my mother to tell her our father had died suddenly in his car in the main street of our town. Apparently some people tried to help but by the time the ambulance got there he'd already died. It was a shock, I can tell you. Even though he had had heart problems all those years, it was still a shock, we just did not expect that he would die so soon.

The immediate tasks

Saying goodbye to the person needs to be done in whatever way you are comfortable with. If a person dies at home, some families prefer not to rush to have the body removed so that goodbyes can be said in familiar surroundings. Saying goodbye can be in the physical presence of the dead person, or doing it mentally whether they are present or not. It is all very much to do with family traditions and your own preferences. The main thing is not to rush into actions that may be regretted later. Ensure that others who also need to say goodbye are given the opportunity, whether at the hospital, at home or at the funeral parlour.

There is one situation which would require swift action after a death and that is if your parent has willed their body or organs for research, transplanting or other purposes. Establish what the dead person had planned and contact the local doctor for advice if your parent died at home or the treating doctor if your parent died in hospital. Also, if your parent died in hospital it may be that you will be asked if the body or some organ can be used for research purposes. If you have not thought about this in advance, it may be hard to make a decision on the spot that you will be satisfied with later on. Just be prepared for this question.

Death certificate and other documents

A medical certificate stating the cause of death can be provided by your parent's usual doctor or a treating doctor at a hospital. The funeral director provides the application for burial or cremation, and the Birth, Death and Marriage Registration form which requires details of the deceased person's birth, parents' names and occupations, marriage details and names and ages of offspring of the deceased.

Later on you will need to complete forms notifying such organisations as Centrelink if the person was a pension or benefit recipient, the Department of Veterans Affairs for veterans, and solicitors, banks and insurance companies. All these organisations will require documented proof of death. You need to find out if they require a certified copy or just a photocopy of the death certificate.

You will need to locate your parent's will which may have some last wishes recorded. If property such as shares is owned in joint names, the ownership passes to the survivor but evidence of the death will need to be produced.

The funeral

It is enormously helpful to a grieving family if the person who has died made plans or at least let people know what they would like to occur at their funeral. This extremely thoughtful act gives the person themselves an opportunity to state their wishes, and greatly eases the burden on their family who are anxious that the funeral will be a fitting tribute to the person who has died. You could encourage your family members to do this, for the comfort of those left behind.

To avoid hasty regrettable decisions, try to ascertain your parents' wishes in advance, at least on the most important decisions:

- Do they want to be buried or cremated?
- Do they wish to be viewed after death?
- Have they offered to donate any body parts for research or other purposes and what are their wishes if you are asked to donate any part of their body after their death?
- Do they want a church service, a funeral chapel service, a service at the crematorium or cemetery only, a memorial service, or perhaps no service?
- Do they want a particular minister or a civil celebrant?
- Are there special club or religious affiliations that need to be considered?
- Would they like to have a family member or a friend giving the eulogy or talking about their life?
- Do they want some gathering held after the funeral or would they prefer a wake or other type of celebration of their life?
- What would they like to be dressed in?
- Would they like to wear their wedding ring or should that be removed and saved for someone in the family?
- Do they want flowers to be sent or people to be asked to make donations to some cause instead?
- What flowers would they like? What cause would they like to support?

- What hymns or music would they like?
- Would they like a memorial book signed by those who attend the funeral?
- What do they wish to be done with the ashes or what wording would they like on their headstone?
- How should the notices in the newspapers be worded?
- Who would they like to be contacted?
- Would they like the thank you cards for condolence messages to be printed, or should you write notes, phone or do nothing?

Choosing the funeral director

Your family may traditionally use a particular firm of undertakers. Some parents may have pre-arranged and even pre-paid their prospective funeral. These days there is a wide variety of options from simple to opulent funerals. There is also a tendency in our competitive society to make inquiries as to options, services and prices. Try not to feel uncomfortable about asking what is included in the prices charged, what the total will be, how much is required prior to the funeral, whether interest will be charged on any outstanding balance, and what the difference is between a coffin and a casket. You may also like to ask:

- How soon after the funeral will a decision have to be made about what to do with the ashes?
- How much will be charged for the flowers that will be in the church or chapel?
- Can they arrange to have all the wreaths set aside somewhere at the crematorium with the cards still attached so they can be collected later?
- How much less will it be if there are not mourning coaches and if family make their own way to the cemetery/crematorium?
- Can a longer time be booked at the chapel at the crematorium, so that people do not have to rush off

because another funeral is coming in? How much extra would this cost?

- Can the funeral be audio and/or video taped for relatives unable to attend?
- Can they guarantee that wedding rings will remain on my parent's finger and come back melted in the ashes?
- If we decide to have a 'viewing', how will they manage that? Will my parent look natural or will they be heavily 'made up'?
- Do their staff stay nearby in case we don't like the viewing and want to leave quickly?

The first few days

It is an exhausting experience to make all the above decisions, which are important and often difficult, to the satisfaction and agreement of what is sometimes a large number of people with differing views. Add the fact that these people may be upset, that you usually may not have much contact with them, and you are coping with your own loss. If there is one parent left, you may be the one physically and emotionally supporting that parent too.

It is important that the principal mourners get as much rest as possible and are given peace and quiet, relieved of answering the phone or responding to queries, and are supported in making decisions. While you may think food is of no significance at this time, it is absolutely essential for helping get through such a stressful, emotional experience. It is great to have someone on hand to keep up a supply of nourishing, comforting food, unobtrusively presented to tempt the grieving person to eat and look after themselves. The other essential is access to the kind of physical, emotional and spiritual support that the person usually finds helpful.

The first few weeks

Whether the death of a parent leaves one parent to be supported or leaves you, or another relative, with the task of winding up the affairs of your parents, the next few weeks will be a busy time. It can also be a stressful time and it is important to care physically for those involved and ensure that they have access to the type of emotional support they value.

Getting on with life

Whether a remaining parent should live alone is a huge question. Leaving their own home may be one of the hardest decisions your parent may have to make. A recently bereaved person is unlikely to be in a position to make a decision which will suit their new circumstances, as they hardly know what life living alone will be like for them. So do not rush these decisions unless there are circumstances that give you no choice.

Painful as it can be, it is often best for the bereaved person to stay in their own home, with support and even someone to stay overnight, while they settle to life without their partner. Some people rush off on holidays 'to forget' and this often only delays the grieving. Staying with family so that physical and emotional support is at hand is good for some people. Whatever your own opinion, it is best to ask your parent what they want to do and then help them to achieve their wishes.

When the time comes to make a decision as to whether your parent should try to continue living in their own home or move somewhere else, you may find it useful to refer to the daily living skills checklist in Chapters 2 and 6 to check the functioning of your remaining parent. You may need to allow for some improvement after the initial shock and grief has passed. Often it is not until one partner dies that the strengths and weaknesses of the other are shown up. Often an old couple will have managed together but neither could manage alone.

Remember that if your surviving parent sells their home, it is final. However, if your parent attempts to continue to live in the home with all the supports available and is still unable to manage, then you all have the satisfaction of having tried your best.

Remembering

Talking about the person who has died, the good and the not so good times, their personality, their rules and attitudes, can bring both tears and laughter. Over time, the talking about the person and times together becomes less painful and can be part of the recovery for the survivors. Some people believe that it is best not to talk about the person who has died and that way everyone will get over it quicker. There may be fewer tears shed, but that is not necessarily a good thing.

Anniversaries can be difficult: wedding anniversaries, birthdays, the first Christmas, Easter and so on. Unfortunately many people tend to act as if there is something magical about the first anniversary of the death, seeing it as the time by which the bereaved partner should be 'over it'. For a long time, for many people, it is more a case of fine one day, sad and lonely the next. Gradually the good days are more frequent. Even so, a person can have some sad grieving days years after the death of a loved one. A thought will spring into their mind and they find themselves tearful. So there is no length of time by which one is 'over it'; the loss just seems to become less of a heartache over time for most people.

What to say, or better still what not to say

A recently bereaved person is likely to have their senses heightened and be sensitive to words or actions which normally would not offend them. But not talking to them for fear of offending or upsetting them is even worse because it is so isolating. This is a time to be a good listener. It can be helpful if you tell the bereaved person that you cannot know how they feel but you can imagine that it must be really awful for them. Ask if they want to talk about how it is for them. Of course it may be that your parent does not want to talk, despite your best listening efforts. In this case, just respect their wish for privacy and be ready to listen at another time.

What not to say is easier. Telling a person that you know exactly how they feel is not helpful, especially as they probably believe you have absolutely no idea how bad it is. Launching into stories of people who have 'got it much worse' is infuriating or extremely discouraging for the bereaved person, even if they patiently listen. Relating the heroic, stoic behaviour of others is equally unhelpful. If someone you love has just died, that is as bad and sad as it gets for you. You do not want to be plied with sadder stories or told how comparatively lucky you are.

Avoidance

Once the activity stops, after the funeral, after seeing people they have not seen for years, and after the first busy weeks immediately following a death, the bereaved person can really begin to feel isolated. People often say that dealing with being avoided by friends is very difficult because they are the very people who could have served as potential company. Some friends avoid talking about the person who has died, although the bereaved people often want to talk about them. Some people physically avoid the bereaved person, crossing the road, pretending not to see, stop phoning, or leave them out of group outings. Such behaviour hurts and confuses and adds to their suffering.

Many people simply avoid someone who is recently bereaved because they find it hard to know what to say to the person. Community health centres, bereavement services and other organisations sometimes present sessions, produce booklets or provide counselling to help people with this very problem. Such services may enable you to be of greater comfort to bereaved friends or relatives.

Expectations of the bereaved parent and yourself

Bereaved people often wonder how long it will be before they start to feel 'themselves' again, or even happy. There is of course no correct answer to this. Sometimes the person who had the most difficult relationship with the deceased takes the most time to recover. Sometimes the person who was closest is able to let go and move on with their lives. It all has to do with feelings of guilt, regret, loss, anger, satisfaction, contentment, and the past relationship with the person who has died.

Being very sad is normal. If someone we loved died and it had little or no effect on us, that would be a disturbing thing. Anger is also a normal response to a death. So is asking, 'Why me' and feeling angry at everyone who still has their partner, angry that the person died and has 'left me in the lurch', angry at the unfairness of it all. 'We had just retired and were looking forward to spending some time together.' It is very important when supporting a grieving person, angry or sad, to let them experience and express their feelings. Avoid trying to jolly them out of it. Avoid trying to convince them they should not be angry. They are sad or angry, or both, and it is best just to allow these feelings and their expression.

If a person really is unable to carry on with life, or if they express a wish to talk to someone outside the family about their loss, counselling by a person skilled in the area of bereavement can be helpful. Such counsellors can be found through community health centres, hospitals, churches and some specific disease or disability organisations. There are also support groups which many people find therapeutic through the sharing of experiences and feelings with other bereaved people. The National Association for Loss and Grief, and Compassionate Friends are two of many such self-help organisations.

The death of a parent is an event which will affect both the immediate and the extended family in some way. It is wise to allow everyone time to adjust. Try to avoid rushing into the big decisions. Be tolerant of different reactions to grief. Remember you will all need time, nurturing and comfort of some kind so try to look out for each other and look after yourself as well.

In conclusion

All over Australia there are people like you, wanting to do something (but not everything!) to help their parents. Now that you have been taken step-by-step through all the considerations to do with your parents getting older, you should feel confident:

- in broaching the subject with them
- in balancing you own and your parents' needs

- in knowing what to expect as your parents age
- about how to help your parents remain as independent as possible
- that you are familiar with the types of help available and know where to find it
- that you will be able to help your parents make wise decisions about their housing and care.

By reading this book, you have taken the first step in equipping yourself and your parents to face the future, even though it may be unpredictable! You have recognised that having ageing parents that you care about will affect your future, and that by thinking and planning ahead, you will be best prepared for the journey together.

Index